When Football Was Fun

(or much ado about nothing-nothing)

By Derek Potter

(Former British Sports Council Reporter of the Year)

EMPIRE
PUBLICATIONS

First published in 2010

EMPIRE PUBLICATIONS
1 Newton Street, Manchester M1 1HW
© Vera Potter 2010

ISBN: 1901746 682 - 9781901746686

Cover design and layout: Ashley Shaw
Edited by Cliff Butler

Printed in Great Britain by KnowledgePoint Ltd.

"Derek didn't spin the news, he reported it,
operating on the basis that there is never
anything so sensational as the truth."

GORDON TAYLOR, CHAIRMAN, PFA.

"He was someone you could trust
implicitly, even though you knew no-one
was quicker to see a good story. He was a
great reporter. He was also a good man."

SIR BOBBY CHARLTON

CONTENTS

EXCLUSIVES

PLAYERS

COLLEAGUES

THE SUMMER GAME

ODDS AND SODS

PREFACE

It is rare that a book is published four years after the passing of the author, but that is the case with 'When Football Was Fun' by Derek Potter.

Derek, who plied his career as a trusted and influential journalist with the *Daily Mirror*, *Daily Express* and *Today*, decided to write the book as a means of 'keeping his hand in' following his retirement from mainstream journalism.

And I am really delighted to say, albeit in a small way, that I was involved in the decision to put his reminiscences and immense store of anecdotes down on paper – or at least filed on his computer.

In my capacity as Manchester United's programme editor I was in the fortunate position of being able to offer Derek the opportunity to work as a contributor on the *United Review*. To have his wonderful writing and depth of football knowledge featuring regularly in the programme was a real coup.

It was a successful association and one that meant we would speak regularly on the telephone. I really enjoyed our little chats and I'm happy to say that it was something that would continue long after he ceased to write for the club.

It was during one of these occasional telephone conversations that Derek would comment that he felt he was 'kicking his heels' and would like something to occupy some of his spare time. I suggested that he should write a book about his memories of the days when football was football.

He scoffed at first saying that no one would be interested in what he had to say. "Are you kidding?" I said. "There is a huge market for nostalgia and the history of the game, people would love to read your stories."

"I'll think about it." he said. In a tone that sounded like he didn't really think it was a good idea.

To my surprise, when we spoke again a few weeks later, he was quick to tell me that he decided to give it a go and that he already done a couple of thousand words and that he was warming to the idea.

It was at that point that I put Derek in contact with Ashley Shaw at Empire Publications. All appeared set for 'When Football Was Fun' to go into print.

We spoke several times after that and he'd just say that he been adding to the manuscript whenever he had the chance.

Then came the distressing news that Derek had passed away soon after returning from a trip to Ireland where he had visited Harry Gregg, the former Manchester United and Northern Ireland goalkeeper, who was a close friend.

Not surprisingly, Derek's funeral was, to put it into football terminology, 'a sell-out'. Such was the number of family, friends, former colleagues, former players and managers, and other football people, that the service had to be relayed to loudspeakers outside in the church grounds. It was a richly-deserved and totally appropriate send-off for a true gentleman of the press.

PREFACE

Some time later Ashley Shaw contacted me at Old Trafford to tell me that Derek's collection of stories were stored on his computer and did I think that it was still possible to go ahead and publish.

I asked Ashley to e-mail the document to me and I said I would take look and get back to him. Imagine my surprise when I opened Derek's text to find that he had amassed in excess of 53,000 words. I had no idea that he had been so busy at his desk. And, of course, it was terrific material as to be expected from a journalist of his calibre.

I called Ashley and said that we should do everything we could to make sure that Derek's efforts were not in vain. He agreed without hesitation and it was decided that between us we would edit and produce the book as a enduring reminder of a fine writer and a true gentleman.

That was more than three years ago and it really is difficult to explain why it took so long to bring the whole project to fruition. Pressure of work, priorities, the financial recession all played a part in delays, but all that really matters is that it has finally happened. Empire Publications' Ashley Shaw and John Ireland and yours truly vowed to Derek's widow, Vera, that we would see the job through and it is on that promise we have delivered.

We are absolutely delighted that the book has finally seen the light of day and as well as providing a lasting epitaph to an outstanding and respected football (and occasionally other sports) journalist it also gives Vera Potter and her family a permanent memento to cherish.

Cliff Butler
Manchester, October 2010

FOREWORD

Derek Potter's story of how it was as a front line and hugely respected reporter through and beyond a great age of English football is certain to evoke the fondest of nostalgia – and a powerful sense of why clubs like Manchester United and Liverpool and men he knew so well, players like Bobby Charlton and Ian St John, exerted such a hold over the imagination of all those who loved the national game.

Because the world has changed so much, along with so many of its values, some of Potter's recall on the following pages reads as though it is coming from another dimension. It is - and this is perhaps its supreme worth and enjoyment.

What we have here, above all else, is not just pure nuggets of wonderful experience, an abiding sense of what it meant to be a reporter who had the ears and the trust of such powerful figures as Sir Matt Busby, Bill Shankly and Don Revie, but also an understanding of why it was possible that a reporter caught between the demands of supplying the voracious needs of a powerful newspaper, mostly a *Daily Express* at the peak of its circulation and influence, and the need not to betray some of the best contacts in the business, should emerge from a long and distinguished career with such a combination of respect and affection.

Potter – or Potty as he was known to many colleagues

long acquainted with his style and puckish, sometimes eccentric humour – trod a difficult line with superb accomplishment and when the pressure did mount, as it would inevitably on a man faced with a relentless requirement to produce exclusive stories, it was absorbed with nothing more self-indulgent than a philosophical shrug.

For anyone who benefited from his kindness and experience, as I did repeatedly as a young reporter at *The Express*, he quickly became more than an esteemed team-mate. He was a friend of unbreakable charm and great patience.

He was a confidante of great names on and off the field but he never surrendered a fierce understanding of his job and the need to exert his own independence.

This was displayed often with great urbanity and the sharpest of wit and one notable victim was his close friend St John, who was at the time entering that tricky phase of all great players when an old turn of speed was beginning to dwindle.

Potter, chasing a deadline, was pursuing Shankly in the corridors of Anfield when he saw St John. "Have you seen Shanks?" Potter asked. St John, who was in one of his more playful moods, gave the reporter mischievous directions but the problem was almost immediately rectified and the player was told, sharply, "Well, it's a long time since you sent someone the wrong way."

Potter chose a professional wrong turning when, shortly after crowning many years of brilliant reporting with the award of sports reporter of the year following a series of exclusives on a Manchester United ownership battle – some things never change – he accepted an offer from the new newspaper *Today*.

Potter, highly valued at *The Express* and at a point in his career when most would have tended to enjoy the comfort of an established reputation, chose a new adventure. It misfired when the new newspaper ran into harsh economic problems and was forced into draconian redundancy measures. Potter was a victim and the manner of his dismissal, which came curtly while he was in the process of filing a deadline report from a football stadium, would have embittered lesser men.

But among his many attributes he had the gift of understanding how the world works – and also an ability to count all the good things it can bring as well as the bad.

Among those gifts, apart from the love of his devoted wife Vera and family, was the ability to do what he liked best and the friendship of so many of those who shaped the game he operated in so professionally for so long.

No-one was a better or more agreeable colleague, a remarkable achievement by someone in a business of often cut-throat competition. Nothing was more dreaded than a late call from a sport desk to say a rival had a powerful exclusive, and nothing was more familiar than the fact that the name Derek Potter was attached to it.

From among his friends and admirers, Sir Bobby Charlton provided one of the finest tributes. He said, "You were always pleased to see Derek Potter; he was someone you could trust implicitly, even though you knew no-one was quicker to see a good story. He was a great reporter. He was also a good man."

In the tough old vineyard of newspapers and professional football no epitaph was better earned.

James Lawton,

Chief sports writer of The Independent.
April 2010

MY FATHER

My father was an inspiration to all he met. A thoughtful, caring and loyal man who would always see the best in everybody. An honest, hardworking family man who never put himself first, even when the chips were down.

Not academically brilliant, by his own admission, but owned a gift and command of the English language that was second to none. This was to be more than proven in his distinguished and respected career as a sports journalist.

He enjoyed life to the full, enjoyed his sport, the odd flutter and a cheeky pint. He has been a tremendous husband, father, grandfather and -friend to us all.

We must all remember him as the fit and active man he was. I for one am honoured to be his son. We all miss him.

Steve

My Dear old "Pop"

A gift very few now possess, belonged to a man with modest desire and a noble understanding of family, this gift of kindness, delightfulness and tranquillity gave hope to others who saw no light in a dark situation. He was my grandpa, and he is a memory worth keeping in all our minds...

"Poppa" – or to the many who know him as "Derek" – provided care and attention throughout his astonishing life, such as the time he insisted on coming to my tennis matches in primary school and was a inspiration even when I did not perform at best.

His fascinating talent with language earned him the respect among the many friends and family he put first before himself, and taught lessons to his curious children, bringing them up to be gentlemen and polite young ladies, which now are skills passed on to his beloved grandchildren that have enabled them to achieve the expectations of his treasured wife and the wise man he is, my loved grandpa, Mr James Potter.

He still lives on in our hearts, and the many who were lucky enough to know him will never forget...

Harry Maule

ACKNOWLEDGEMENTS

Thanks to the thousands of footballers and cricketers for providing me with so much to enjoy and so much to write about; thanks, too, to my family and special friends for their tolerance of erratic hours, if not erratic behaviour, and to my learned colleagues on the *Daily Express* and other publications for their encouragement and guidance.

All illustrations in the publication are reproduced by kind permission of the Express Newspapers.

The author apologises to students of English for grammatical transgressions and to statisticians for factual errors.

MANAGERS

BUSBY POACHED TO JOIN UNITED

SIR MATT BUSBY, morally if not illegally poached by Manchester United from Liverpool, fired the first salvos in a soccer revolution that was to launch the game from its enforced wartime slumber into the tactical and financial jungle where success became paramount and entertainment was frequently relegated to become a modest secondary consideration.

Progress was slow at first as power in the game changed direction, eventually to the detriment of the less financially-powerful clubs left struggling to survive in what became a soccer jungle. From being under-paid lackeys, the players eventually emerged to become the power force in the game by 2000 or before.

Sir Matt was later the key figure in another blatant "tapping" incident that went unchallenged by authority and took Denis Law to Old Trafford in a surge of glory for player and club. Such blatant flouting of the game's rules would not have avoided close scrutiny later as Chelsea, among others, were to find out. Sir Matt led soccer's industrial revolution and made the first inroads into the domination of interfering directors' box bullies, many of whom believed they knew more about the game than the man they had chosen to be in charge. The players increased the pace of reform when they forced a re-think on pay when they smashed the minimum wage structure in 1961.

Busby's stand came early in his career as a rookie manager when as a 35-year-old he overheard a director question his tactical know-how. "Never dare to say anything like that to me again when other people can hear you," he demanded. And to strengthen his case, he formally asked the club chairman to confirm he had a free hand on all playing matters.

Busby, who joined Liverpool in 1936 from Manchester City to become one of the many 'litmus' transfers between Maine Road and Old Trafford, was given that assurance.

The emphasis on having a strong nursery system – the "Busby Babes" – was a blueprint first envisaged by Wolves before the war that other clubs were eager to copy with varying success and still do. Several months before the end of the war when he latterly ran a team of all-stars to entertain the troops, Sir Matt was outrageously "tapped" on the clubs' behalf by an old friend, Louis Rocca, the club's chief scout. "I could not trust any letter going to Liverpool (FC)," Rocca wrote. "I have a great job for you. Please get in touch with me at the above address." In his book, 'Soccer at the Top' Sir Matt admitted: "I could have played on for another year or two at Anfield and then perhaps taken a staff job there."

The Busby dream was in turn to become an age of glory, then a depressing nightmare and ultimately a triumph in the European Cup in 1968, one year after the triumph by Glasgow Celtic under the distinguished baton of Jock Stein. Busby set standards, developed trends and had much influence on the game's renaissance from the material austerity of wartime and its carefree, vastly entertaining form of football, towards the lavish expenditure and economics strategy that made the superstructure perilously top heavy and in danger of collapse. Football for fun rapidly became football for finance with Chelsea setting a new and dangerous trend leaving rivals struggling in their slipstream on the pitch and floundering in the financial whirlwind.

THE DAY A TEAM DIED

NO FAN NOR any journalist will ever forget where they were or what they were doing the day a team died. It was an event far beyond the level of petty jealousies or illogical prejudices. News travelled slowly (relatively, that is, in 1958) but through a contact and a freak telephone call, I was among the first Mancunians to hear that the plane carrying Manchester United home from a mission in Europe, had crashed on a third attempted take-off at Munich Airport. I dashed off ahead of my designated shift at the *Daily Mirror* office in Manchester where I then worked as a general news sub-editor.

By the time I arrived, the office was already jammed with journalists who had also either come in early, or stayed on after their shift, to help in the production of the paper's flow of special editions, and to hear, at first hand, bulletins from the Rechts der Isar Hospital, Munich.

A city's grief was shared by the nation and beyond. It is doubtful that a similar tragedy then to Chelsea, Arsenal, Liverpool or Newcastle United would have generated quite such a flow of nationwide sympathy. United were the darlings of their day, built on the success of a flow of home produced players in a prolific academy.

It is impossible to put a price on the value of the soccer starlets who perished or were injured when their plane crashed after a re-fuelling stop on the way home from Belgrade. The United "Babes" had won the League in 1955-56 by eleven points and again the following season. United, or rather more accurately Sir Matt himself, had defied the authorities by becoming the first English team to venture into Europe. He strongly believed that the development of British football would be enhanced by the experience of playing on the Continent.

Glasgow Celtic were to head off Busby's dream of becoming the first British European champions by one year, beating Inter Milan 2-1 in Lisbon from where one inebriated fan was smuggled back on an aircraft to Glasgow by friends, only to reveal on his arrival that his car was back in Lisbon! Chelsea had toed the political line by declining the chance to go into Europe after winning the title in 1954-55, a feat they were destined not to repeat for another 50 years. An amazing, if unpalatable, statistic for the Stamford Bridge HQ, considering the later successes of Liverpool, Manchester United, Nottingham Forest and Aston Villa.

Suffice to say that the team that died at Munich was some way off reaching its peak. Even so, many players had reached international status. The full-backs Billy Foulkes and Roger Byrne were England players. Eddie Colman, another product of the system, was raising eyebrows at his audacious hip-waggling play as a wing half. Jackie

Blanchflower was an Northern Ireland defender, Mark Jones was a solid centre half, Duncan Edwards was the boy (aged 18, that is) who played like a man with an amazing flourish and a vast range of playing assets. Liam Whelan was a smooth-playing Republic of Ireland "general."

Dennis Viollet was later to play for England and David Pegg had already apeared on the wing for England. Bobby Charlton was just getting into the first team reckoning – a process that was rapidly and unhappily speeded by the crash. There were also fringe players of the quality of Geoff Bent, Nobby Stiles, Johnny Giles, Nobby Lawton, Alex Dawson and Mark Pearson. It would be impossible to even guess at the worth of those players in the grossly inflated talent market that emerged towards the end of the twentieth century. Eight United players, three of the club's staff and eight of the nine newspapermen on board were fatally injured on February 6, 1958.

Sir Matt himself was severely injured. He had been in mental turmoil on the tarmac desperate for a successful third take-off, knowing that failure to return to England on schedule to fulfil the week-end fixture against Wolves would bring the sternest censure from the English football authorities, openly hostile to the European venture.

"Who was I?" Sir Matt reflected, "to presume to tell an expert pilot how to do his job? I certainly knew less about than aeroplanes that he knew about football." A team that with an average age of about 21 won the 1956 title was destroyed.

The peak performance was probably beating

Anderlecht 10-0 in their first European home tie, played at Maine Road! Why Maine Road? Well, City had one up on United in the floodlighting department. It was not until the semi-final against Real Madrid – after playing Anderlecht, Borussia, and Bilbao "away" in Moss Side – that the lights had gone up at Old Trafford.

Beside the loss of footballing talent, the cream of the North's football writers perished in the crash: the pipe-smoking Alf Clarke (*Manchester Evening Chronicle*), Donnie Davies (*Manchester Guardian*), George Follows (*Daily Herald*), Tom Jackson (*Manchester Evening News*), Archie Ledbrooke (*Daily Mirror*), Henry Rose (*Daily Express*), and Eric Thompson (*Daily Mail*).

They all had different styles. For instance, Eric Thompson would be as busy with his sketchbook as his notebook drawing cartoons to go with his reports and their departure left a tremendous gap to be filled, albeit minor compared with the re-building job that faced an asset-stripped United. Frank Swift, the former Manchester City and England goalkeeper with massive hands and a huge heart, representing the *News of the World*, also perished. Frank Taylor (*News Chronicle*), though badly injured, was the only reporter to survive.

Harry Gregg, signed from Doncaster Rovers late in 1957, Charlton, Viollet, Foulkes, Albert Scanlon and Kenny Morgans were the players to survive the crash on the way home from drawing with Red Star of Belgrade, with United claiming to a place in the European Cup semi-final with a berth in the fifth round of the F.A. Cup already won and the team running second in the League.

United also lost the backbone of their staff in Walter Crickmer, the secretary, and coaches Tom Curry and Bert Whalley. After convalescence, Sir Matt and his loyal assistant Jimmy Murphy set about re-building the team. Albert Quixall was signed from Sheffield Wednesday for £45,000 and, astonishingly, United finished the 1958-59 season as runners up to Stan Cullis's rampaging Wolves. On Bobby Charlton's say-so, Sir Matt signed the fiery Maurice Setters for £30,000.

Later, Noel , a versatile defender was signed from West Ham for £29,500 to boost the re-building operation. Sir Matt strove to keep the glamour image of United alive and arranged a friendly against Real Madrid, winners, incredibly of the first five years of the European Cup Sir Matt dreamed of winning, from 1956. Matt met the Real president Santiago Bernabeu – the Real Madrid stadium bears his name to this day - and he agreed to bring his famous Kings of the Football World to Old Trafford for a friendly.

The former European masters normally commanded a fee of about £12,000 to play friendlies. Real's gesture to the stricken club, in slashing the fee by half, underlined the depth of feeling that surged across the Continent and the globe. Then Real walloped United 6-1! The margin of that defeat underlined the huge re-building task facing United. It is doubtful if any other club could have survived such a massive setback and re-emerge so formidably.

A little anecdote sums up the extent of the emotional surge of sympathy for United and their plight. Henry Rose was among the nine journalists who perished with

11 United players and staff. On the day of the funeral of the popular reporter and broadcaster – a speech impediment that became almost a broadcasting trade mark announcing himself as Henry "Wose" added to his charisma - taxis were lined up outside the *Daily Express* office in Great Ancoats Street to take mourners to the synagogue for Henry's funeral. The drivers offered their cabs free, in touching memory of the man who had communicated with the masses, using extraordinary journalistic gimmicks.

Henry's technique was unique. "If Tommy Taylor is England's centre forward, I'm Father Christmas," he once wrote, already knowing from a trusted insider that the Manchester United centre forward – Busby paid Barnsley £29,999 to avoid the pressure of the £30,000 pricetag - had *already* been picked to make his debut in the forthcoming England match. Alongside the text announcing Taylor's elevation to international status, was a picture of Rose in a Father Christmas outfit!

MURPHY'S LAW

JIMMY MURPHY, Matt Busby's loyal assistant at Old Trafford, was the manager's first 'signing' for United when they met behind the front line in Italy towards the end of the war. "Give me a ring when we're demobbed," pleaded Busby. Murphy and Busby blended with complete confidence one with the other. "Jimmy would always give me a straightforward opinion," Sir Matt recalled in his book 'Soccer at the Top'. "Jimmy was never a 'yes' man. But once I made a decision he would accept it. There was never a suggestion of usurping my position."

The combination of Busby's brains and Murphy's muscle was the foundation of United's re-birth at Old Trafford, badly damaged by enemy bombs early in the war. Murphy, even as manager of Wales, was happier in the background. That changed when Murphy took the helm as Sir Matt recovered from his extensive injuries sustained in the Munich air crash. Jimmy had not flown with the team to Belgrade, staying behind to take charge at Old Trafford. It was a crucial phase in the club's history. Murphy assembled and inspired an all-sorts team good enough to beat Sheffield Wednesday, West Brom and Fulham to reach the F.A. Cup Final against Bolton.

Only a controversial goal by Nat Lofthouse, when he barged goalkeeper Harry Gregg and the ball over his goal-line, robbed Murphy's men of the chance of repeating the Wembley success in the tournament a decade earlier. Murphy's team included the specially-registered Stan Crowther who, he had recalled, had shone in mid-field for Aston Villa who beat United 2-1 in the Final of 1957. Crowther uniquely played for two teams in the same F.A. cup competition. Ernie Taylor, a tactical genius, was signed to blend with Crowther's bite and drafted into mid-field to add a creative spark. With the nation behind them, United lost 2-0.

The quality of the team, despite losing its main components at Munich, is self-evident in the line-up: Gregg; Foulkes, Greaves; Goodwin (also a cricketer with Lancashire), Cope, Crowther; Dawson, Taylor (E), Charlton, Viollet, Webster. Murphy played a major, and sometimes underestimated, role in the post war history of

United, being the iron first to blend with Busby's velvet glove. An example of Murphy's attention to detail was his approach to Bobby Charlton. Murphy recognised the youngsters power and potential. "Bobby," urged Murphy, "you need to be two-footed." Charlton took the hint and after every training session he would bang the ball with his left foot against a brick wall at ever-increasing range. The rest, as they say, is football history.

My first meeting with Murphy was memorable. Anxious to establish a rapport with the man I only "knew" from the newspapers, I introduced myself. "Hello, Mr. Murphy," I said hand outstretched. It must have been a bad day.

"Nice to meet you," he growled, brushing my outstretched hand. "I like your approach – now let's see your departure. Buzz off." We developed a firm friendship after that dodgy first meeting, with me often succeeding where others had failed, in persuading Jimmy to publically display his skills at the piano.

BIG BOOTS TO FILL

RON ATKINSON, who I once saved from a potential social disaster during his colourful years at Manchester United, inadvertently wrecked his lucrative, high profile career on the box. It took even the resilient Ron some time to repair the damage of his off-mike jibe at Marcel Desailly with a serious racist gaffe that was inadvertently broadcast live in the Middle East; serious, that is, to those who were unaware that Atkinson is "colour blind" and had previously encouraged and developed many black players. Atkinson immediately quit his £200,000 a year job with ITV. Those who knew and liked him, were always aware that Big Ron had a Scouser's sense of humour, often leaning heavily on wicked self-deprecating sarcasm frequently open to wrongful interpretation by the super-sensitive.

It was in Madrid on a player signing mission accompanied by his second wife Maggie that Atkinson escaped a potential embarrassment thanks to my SOS. He and Maggie were among a group of football people when a photographer going about his job, turned his lens on the attractive, dusky Maggie and Ron. Instinctively I grabbed the nearest phone and shouted out: "Maggie – it's a call for you," inviting her out of range to take a non-existent call. It seemed that to be photographed with Maggie while still married to his first, equally pleasant wife Margaret, was a needless possible complication.

Towards the end of his year in exile (2005), Ron was invited in from the cold by TV station Bravo for their coverage of Italian football. Bravo's hope was to recapture the fans who enjoyed Channel 4's coverage of Serie A games. Atkinson had previously covered Premiership games for Scandanavian and other outlets and written a column for the *Sunday Sport* before it was a case of bravo to Bravo for welcoming him back on the big screen. Atkinson's debut was with a former player he knew well, Lee Sharpe formerly of Manchester United and a star of Celebrity Love Island. "I've done some reality TV myself," Atkinson said. "I've been off to Provence with Esther Rantzen and Marcus Brigstock to learn French and be set tasks." Atkinson did not argue that one challenge to run a restaurant for the day turned out more like a scene from 'Allo "Allo."

We knew (didn't we?) that Big Ron would return to football eventually and he did half way through season 2005-6.We should have guessed, too, at the circumstances; a lowly club with a rookie black manager in charge. His mission as a consultant was to use his expertise and contacts to help Iffy Onuora in his formidable task of keeping Swindon in League One. Onuora needed help after his 17 games in charge yielded only four wins, seven draws and six defeats "I won't be stepping on the manager's toes – I hope he will use my experience," Atkinson said. Involvement with a newly-formed NW One television company was not to Onuora's liking and a switch was planned to promotion-chasing Peterborough whose director of football, Barry Fry is a friend of Atkinson's.

Ron savoured two F.A. Cup wins while at Manchester United, who dismissed him in 1986 despite having never finished lower than fourth place in the senior league. At West Brom he had three black players under his command, Laurie Cunningham, Cyrille Regis and Brendon Batson who he humorously called the 'Three Degrees'. Manchester United often relied on a potent attack to disguise holes, permanent or temporary, in defence.

Sir Matt always encouraged a cavalier style, illustrated perfectly in a match against Middlesbrough at Ayresome Park where United were four (I think) goals down by half time. A former colleague Peter Thomas, whose father and uncle were on the board, smiled across the room at half time his expression and thumbs up clearly indicating that he expected a notable victory. Thomas senior nodded back with an anxious look."Its Manchester we're playing, son" he cautioned. United won 5-4.

One of the many gems Sir Matt inherited when he and Jimmy Murphy assumed command was John Carey, a pipe-smoking genial Irishman who never seemed to be in a hurry on or off the pitch. Carey resumed his career after the war at inside right. Gradually, Sir Matt shuffled him through the team utilising his talents where he believed there were potential weaknesses. Eventually, Carey "retreated" to right back where he captained United and the Republic of Ireland with skill and poise. Carey wore ten of the 11 shirts for United in League games during his glittering career as a player. Many pints have been won on the question: "Which shirt did John Carey never wear for United." All but those with an intimate knowledge of United in those carefree days would presume that he never played in goal. He did, several times. With distinction, of course. Carey's move into management was ended when he was axed as manager of Everton by the chairman Sir John Moores during a taxi ride.

Many supporters and fans lucky enough to witness his precocious talent, firmly believed that Duncan Edwards had the talent,physique and temperament to become *the* greatest player of all time had he not so cruelly become a victim of the Munich crash in 1958. The son of Dudley in Worcestershire, was only 16 when he made his League debut for United. The next year he played in England's first Under-23 international team and then aged 18 years and 183 days won the first of his 18 caps. "He seemed too good to be true – we couldn't find a fault in him;

he was a Colossus first among the boys and then among the men," was Busby's summing up in his book, "Soccer At The Top."

My own challenger for Mr.Versatility of soccer would go to Bryan Robson. It takes courage as well as skill to be labelled the best defender, most creative mid-fielder, and most potent striker as he was in one Manchester United game. The title of Captain Marvel was well earned and well deserved by a player who broke a leg three times inside a year at West Brom where he began his career and then masterminded the Great Escape as manager in the compelling drama of May 2005. Robson rated that escape at West Brom as his greatest achievement, surpassing even the hat-trick he scored for England and the fastest-ever World Cup goal in 27 seconds.

Robson was undoubtedly Ron Atkinson's most successful signing and definitely the vital tool in the hands of Sir Alex Ferguson, more valuable for his versatility and example on the pitch until the emergence of the inspiring Roy Keane and Eric Cantona. The amazing consistency and sure-footed tackling of Denis Irwin, stolen by Ferguson from Oldham Athletic for £650,000 after being discarded by Leeds United, was another hugely successful coup. A year after being snatched from Boundary Park, Irwin won the first of his 56 caps for the Republic of Ireland. His performance graph rarely soared; it just as surely rarely dipped. I rated him the most consistent performer I had seen since Alan Oakes of Manchester City and arguably one of the most prudent and successful transfers in many years.

Atkinson's signing of Robson could easily be

considered even more prudent, in that he signed three players and an inspirational captain in one package. The ambitious Atkinson may well have found his results disappointing at Old Trafford. The acquisition of Robson was handsomely rewarded at Old Trafford, once branded "Cold Trafford" in a *Daily Express* headline during the reign of the highly intelligent, if introverted, Dave Sexton who later extended his studies to Master's level. Sexton's honesty did not make him an ideal candidate for the cut and mistrust developing in the game, though his integrity was intact to the end when his temperament and driving skills were tested as he drove away from Old Trafford after his sacking, narrowly missing myself and a colleague as he raced red-faced out of the car park and eventually on to the pay roll at the F.A..

The staid but totally honest Sexton, who served sherry at his Friday media conferences while other managers often dispensed vitriol or humour, did not deserve the disrespect accorded to him. That, perhaps, peaked over the signing of Ray Wilkins. "I've just signed Ray Wilkins – but don't tell the manager," confided Louis Edwards, the pork butcher's son who once worked in his dad's shop, as he beckoned me to his breakfast table during a pre-season tour in Scandanavia. "I'll announce it later." Edwards was a bluff-spoken but highly numerate chairman of Manchester United; a man you ignored at your peril.

The prelude to the departure of Frank O'Farrell was embarrassing and painful for colleague Jimmy Mossop, then of the *Sunday Express*. A small gathering including Bobby Charlton, Alex Stepney, the chairman Louis

Edwards, Sir Matt, Mossop and I, were enjoying a quiet chat in the summer of 1972 at the team's pre-season HQ in a Berlin suburb. O'Farrell, lamb to the lion of Tommy Docherty, strode red-faced and angry-looking towards the group brandishing a copy of the *Sunday Express*. In it were extensive quotes from an informant and inside 'gen' about United in Mossop's column. O'Farrell swung the paper across Mossop's cheek. Shocked, he rose to his feet and confronted O'Farrell. I pushed Jim back into his chair. It was all over in seconds. The players vanished, moving quicker than at any time in their playing careers. Sir Matt Busby inquired: "What was all that about?" though it was suspected that he had already guessed. Mossop, banned from travelling with the team for the rest of the tour, and I vanished to the sanctuary of another bar. Before Christmas the likeable fish out of water O'Farrell was job-hunting, having sent Mossop a card "hoping the cold war is over".

Many managers studied the management technique of Busby and others of his generation, some more successfully than others it must be said, certainly not the boss who demanded "more harmonium" in the dressing room at half time. Sir Alex and Ron Atkinson were masters of knowing when to pat a player on the back or when to kick him up the backside; the carrot and stick technique. Many managers followed Sir Matt's trick of cleverly using the knowledge of others to solve his own problems. This quality was often emphasised in mixed company: players, club officials, media. Matt would sidle alongside someone he knew who would know the answer and enquire: "What's the name of that young player/director/reporter over there?" Thus furnished with the answer (often in confirmation of his suspicion, anyway), Matt would extend his hand and offer a friendly greeting to, say, Joe Bloggs, or Fred Fanakapan. He had a remarkable memory for names, faces and incidents.

TREND SETTERS

IF SIR MATT BUSBY was a trend setter, a series of managers took his lead - honing and improving the 'art' of management towards the 21st century for better or for worse. Busby was a pioneer, flouting authority and taking United into Europe against the wishes of an establishment wary of involvement in football on the continent and largely dominated by an inward-looking hierarchy.

It follows, therefore, that it was Sir Matt's dream to become the first winners of the European Cup, a crusade that was to lead to the tragedy of Munich. United achieved Sir Matt's dream a year after Glasgow Celtic won the crown in 1967. Manchester United overpowered Benfica in exciting style at Wembley, fully utilising the "home" advantage of a 100,000 strong crowd.

The sixties era had seen the emergence of super slick Spurs under the direction of Bill Nicholson who paired the creativity of Danny Blanchflower with the power of Dave Mackay at the fulcrum of the first team in the twentieth century to win the League and Cup double in 1961. Spurs, incidentally, have the rather unusual distinction of being the only team to win the F.A. Cup as a non-League club. The seemingly impossible happened in 1901 when Spurs from the Southern League drew

2-2 with Sheffield United at Crystal Palace and won the replay 3-1 at Burnden Park, Bolton. Spurs, incidently, were the first British club to win a European trophy, beating the holders Atletico Madrid in Rotterdam by the impressive margin of 5-1 in 1963 to clinch the Cup Winners' Cup.

Teams came and went. Liverpool thundered on, United then Arsenal dominated and then there was Derby County and Nottingham Forest under the remarkable baton of Brian Clough, arguably a rival to any of the managerial giants since football for fun became football for finance.

Cloughie, it can be claimed, was an amalgam of managers, combining the carrot and stick approach of Sir Matt Busby, the humour of Joe Mercer, the detailed determination of Don Revie, the silken touch of Bill Nicholson, the cunning of Arsene Wenger, the guile of Martin O'Neill (one of Clough's chief lieutenants in the field of combat), the all-embracing talents of Sir Alex Ferguson and the single-minded grit of a third knight, Sir Alf Ramsey. There was also the strength of Stan Cullis and Jock Stein who did so much for Wolves and Glasgow Celtic respectively.

Needless to say, his style did not always win Clough friends in high places. "I'm sure the England selectors thought if they took me on and gave me the manager's job, I'd want to run the show," he recalled. "They were shrewd. Because that's exactly what I would have done."

The public adored him, especially in the East Midlands where he was a freeman of both Derby and

Nottingham who petitioned for him to join the list of soccer knights. Most players respected Clough for his rough, engaging leadership. He won championships with Derby and Forest and brought two European Cups to Nottingham with teams that had a silky quality and could rival any produced in England since the Second World War.

Clough once visited a sick colleague in a Midlands nursing home. After flouncing in to the private ward (clutching a bottle of champagne), Clough left after administering a mental pep talk, noting that there was no TV set in the room. Next day, a new TV arrived – compliments of Cloughie.

Goals did the talking for Cloughie during his playing days – 251 in 274 League games mainly in the second division with Middlesbrough. He was never stuck for words when he moved into management with Hartlepool. Although words can barely describe the turbulent 44 days spent as manager of Leeds United. Revie, who had joined Leeds in 1961 and quit to become manager of England on July 4 1974, was a hard act to follow even for a manager as capable and experienced as Clough, who, it was said, always had a bottle of his favourite tipple hidden among the brambles for refreshment during his gardening stints.

Revie had hauled the Elland Road club by its bootlaces from the wrong end of the old Second Division to a place among the masters of European football, winning the League championship twice, the F.A. Cup and the Inter Cities Fairs Cup twice. They were probably at their peak when they won a second title in 1974 when

Revie chose to leave with his ambition of winning the European Cup still a dream away.

"Revie certainly did not believe Brian Clough was the right man to finish the job when he was surprisingly named as his successor," recalled Jimmy Armfield the former captain of England and Blackpool in his autobiography *Right Back to the Beginning.* "I often wondered if Revie left because he simply couldn't bear to break up his football family himself."

Revie took his assistant Les Cocker, with him to the F.A. and Clough appointed Jimmy Gordon as his assistant. Clough also imported two of his field marshals from Derby, midfielder John McGovern and striker John O'Hare for a combined fee of £125,000, peanuts by later escalating standards. He then bought the dazzling and often baffling striker Duncan McKenzie from Nottingham Forest for £250,000. Clough told Eddie Gray, a talented and popular player at Elland Road who had endured a series of major injuries: "If you were a racehorse, you would have been put down."

Things started badly, as they say, and rapidly fell away. Leeds played nine League and cup games in Clough's stormy 44 days and won just one. "The club was in a mess," recalled Armfield with a degree of understatement when he succeeded Clough at Elland Road where the championship flag still flew.

THE MAGYAR REVOLUTION

FOOTBALL IN ENGLAND was shaken and stirred by the Hungarians who inspired a tactical revolution at Manchester City. They walloped England 6-3 to become the first successful invaders at Wembley in 1953 where a year earlier Newcastle United had become the first club to win the F.A. Cup in successive seasons in the 20th century. It was definitely back to the drawing board a year later when England were crushed 7-1 in the Nep Stadium, Budapest. Not only did the result ricochet round the F.A.'s headquarters. A remarkable by-product of the revolution inspired by the blatantly one-footed Puskas and the deep-lying Hidegkuti was hatched over a "fag and a cup of tea" in the tiny boot room under the Maine Road main stand. Physio Laurie Barnet and former centre-forward Fred Tilson, who had scored twice in the 1934 Cup success over Portsmouth to avenge defeat by Everton a year earlier, laid the tactical foundations. The Revie Plan was conceived.

Manchester City manager Les McDowall embellished the tactical revolution, using Johnny Williamson in the Revie role at reserve team level. The Plan was ready for take off without Williamson, the guinea pig who became a lifelong friend of Revie's, the deep-lying creative centre forward. There were many tactical hiccups in the attempts to capitalise on the long-ranging and space-finding passes of Revie, regarded by many as lacking the pace to be a frontrunner, behind players grappling to adapt to the newness of their revolutionary system. In front were permutations of Johnny Hart, a sharp and sleek scorer, Bobby Johnstone, a caresser of the ball, the strong-running Joe Hayes, wingers Roy Clarke, Paddy Fagan, Billy Spurdle, Ken Marsden and Jack Dyson, also a first class cricketer.

Despite nerve-testing defeats and doubts on the terraces and inside the boardroom, McDowall had the courage and conviction to press on with the Revie Plan. Even defeat by the mighty Newcastle United in the 1955 F.A. Cup Final failed to induce a notion of failure. City returned in tactical triumph to Wembley the following year thanks to the probing Revie and the work rate of those 'off the ball'. This time, City triumphed but not without a banana skin escapade that was to become part of the club's folklore.

Goals from Hayes, Dyson and Johnston crushed Birmingham City who could only beat goalkeeper Bert Trautmann once, despite the popular and spectacular giant former German paratrooper playing half of the the final with a broken neck. Apart from the occasional rub and grimace of pain, Bert played the rest of the game as if nothing unusual had happened. Such a contrast to recent years when even a minor nudge has merited six forward rolls, face distorted in agony and head buried in the turf. It was said that Trautmann, a former PoW who soon became accepted as an honoured guest in Manchester, was obliged to hack his long blond hair short to reduce his sex appeal!

City always seem to be the masters of the unpredictable, winning matches as 6-1 outsiders or even greater odds, and losing when odds-on favourites. It seemed to be a tradition that City shredded the form book even before the ink was dry. "Batty Blues" should be City's motto; they have always been a good club though and brave warriors in the red shadow of Manchester United for decades. City hold an amazing scoring record as the only club to score and concede a century of goals in a season. City hit 104 and leaked 100 in finishing fifth in 1957/58.

City's about-turn in the Second Division play-off final against Gillingham in 1999 was typical. The blues were so down and apparently out, in a game that had begun with them odds-on favourites, that thousands of supporters were seen streaming away from Wembley and heading homewards with City trailing 2-0 until they heard the roar that told them City were back in the game and on their way to a stunning success and promotion alongside Fulham and Walsall.

The snatching of victory from the jaws of defeat (many writers before and since have churned out what became a cliché of 'snatching defeat from the jaws of victory') underlined City's traditional habit of tearing up their own form book.

★

NOT SURPRISINGLY Revie, the deep-lying centre forward, became Revie the deep-thinking manager, with quite spectacular success at Leeds United. He blended, coaxed, bullied, dominated and demanded devotion to his plan for success at home and abroad. Jack Charton – he always called him Revie, never boss or Mr. Revie or Don – owes his ultimate success at international level and the joy of being centre-half in the team with his brother

Bobby that won the World Cup in 1966 under Sir Alf "wingless wonders" Ramsey, to his club manager.;

"I used to argue with Revie about the style and role I should play at Leeds," recalled Big Jack, who became a national hero in the Republic of Ireland with his management at World Cup level, and his rapport with the Irish grew in proportion with amount of fish he caught in that nation's rivers.

"Éventually it dawned on me almost at the point of my despair at ever playing as well as I knew I could and should, that Revie was right after all. I had come close to wrecking my career."

Revie's team plan with Leeds United was rigid off the field as well as on it. Players were subjected to games of indoor bowls and quizzes as diversions from the tension of games. Abroad after matches, players were ushered into a convenient room to ensure they were not attracted by the dazzling lights outside the team hotel. Billy Bremner, an uncompromising wing half and charmer off the pitch, was 'Master of Ceremonies' at such social events and Charlton was in charge of liquid refreshments.

Jack would stride round the room asking "What's yours, Johnny, Norman, Paul?" Lord Harewood, the Queen's cousin and President of the club, was in the company and next in line. Without consciously pondering the appropriate form of address, Big Jack inquired, "And what's yours, George?".

"I'll have a beer, thanks Jack," replied Lord Harewood. They became firm friends, sharing a liking for country life and fishing.

One of Bremner's duties at these after-match functions was to point with his master's baton to a player or member of staff who was expected to provide some form of entertainment, usually a joke or charade. Bremner, of course, pointed at Lord Harewood. His Lordship responded with a lively impersonation of royalty being introduced to the restless lines of Cup Final players before the kick-off, walking past an imaginary team offering his hand and being greeted by a stationary jogger, a player performing leg stretches with one hand behind his back or a player bent double in the process of a toe-touching routine while others fidgited from leg to leg. Lord Harewood's performance was rated one of the best at the Revie gatherings. Bremner, incidentally, could be as sharp with his tongue as he was with his feet in a tackle. He once said to my colleague Alan Thompson, who was awaiting radical dental treatment: "Tommo, you've got teeth like a row of condemned hooses (houses)." Both revelled in the joke.

It was often claimed that Revie declined to let his team off the leash, tactically that is, for they certainly were not discouraged to be a physical as well as a creative team. It was felt by many that Leeds should have exceeded their achievements at home and abroad. Slender success in the old Fairs Cup (1-0) over the two legs against Ferencvaros in 1968 was followed by failure in a personally memorable final against AC Milan five years later.

Salonika was the setting and on arrival in Greece, I sought the whereabouts of Wilf McGuinness then working as coach to Aris Salonika after a disastrous spell as successor to the "irreplaceable" Sir Matt Busby at Manchester United. An old football pal Les Shannon warned me when we arrived in Greece: "Don't look surprised when you meet Wilf." I was surprised, no shocked, to see that the old black-haired wing half warrior had lost his hair in a bout of alopecia brought on by his shock departure from Old Trafford where he had served United man and (Busby) babe.

Far from being coy or embarrassed, McGuinness was up-front about his overnight hair loss and made jokes about his sunburned head. He wore an outrageous black wig when he sat on the touchline for a game in the baking sun. When his striker missed an open goal when it looked easier to score, Wilf flung his wig into the dust in disgust and theatrically trampled it with both feet. After a while, McGuinness felt the sun burn into his unprotected head. Sheepishly, he retrieved the forgotten wig, shook off the dust, and plonked it back on his head without a glance to friend or foe.

McGuinness was later to use that story in his after dinner addresses and revelled about how he once screamed at George Best during a game. "Pass to Bobby, he's in the clear". Best sped on, ball at his feet. "Oh hells bells, lob it to Denis, he's moving in unmarked at the far post." George still had the ball. "You nutter, George, cross it now, NOW. Give it. GIVE IT NOW. Bloody hell George…what a f★★★ing goal."

That visit to Greece had begun in an unusual and unrewarding way. The night before departure, I discussed with a close and well-informed Leeds contact a story I was checking that Everton were desperate to sign Revie as their manager to succeed Harry Catterick who had recently retired. I knew that the nod at long range from my Leeds contact when we arrived for departure at Ringway Airport, Manchester, the next morning was confirmation that my story was definitely on. I wrote my yarn in less than perfect Pitman's ready to phone my exclusive on arrival in Greece. But a rival reporter looking over my shoulder from the row of aircraft seats behind mine somehow managed to interpret my scraggy shorthand. The story was out. Every reporter used it, except the man from *The Sun* who had decoded my dodgy Pitmans and who insisted my "scoop" was a fair cop. "It's your story – I'm not using it," he said.

A similar scoop of considerable impact happened when Robert Maxwell, the bluff and later disgraced publisher, made a bid to take over Manchester United, some years before the successful coup by Malcolm Glazer. Maxwell returned my call and without giving me chance to expand, gruffly told me: "There's no story" and hung up. That response convinced me that there *was* a story. Days of playing a waiting game, including telephone calls to a valued contact in the Middle East, made me confident to reveal the move by Maxwell. Days later I was able to exclusively reveal that the deal was doomed. Three words from an insider gave the *Express* a prestige exclusive: "The bid fails."

SHANKLY STORMS ANFIELD

BILL SHANKLY'S arrival at Liverpool saw his genius, eccentricity and a measure of luck write a success story that swept across Merseyside, the domestic game and deep into Europe.

Shankly's good fortune was in inheriting Bob Paisley at Anfield. Their chemistry was unique, founded on mutual respect and trust. If Paisley had an input, big or small, to make about an individual player or the team, he quickly discovered a clever way of feeding it into the Shankly think-tank.

"I would suggest something to Bill who I knew would always listen to me," Paisley once told me. "Often he would reply 'nae Bob, nae' at my input, and a week later after poo-pooing my suggestion, it would be introduced into training as Bill's idea. In that way we were both happy. If he didn't agree with me neither of us would mention it again."

The honours board at Anfield traces the successes during the Shankly era with the subsequent regimes of Paisley himself (reluctantly) and Joe Fagan (even more reluctantly) who with Reuben Bennett and Roy Evans and other later recruits comprised arguably the strongest boot room hierarchy in Europe.

Shanks, a stabbing two-fingered typist who managed without the services of a secretary, was massively complex and utterly devoted to his craft. Once, one early morning the day after one of Liverpool's early ventures into European football, Shanks glanced at a headline in a Continental edition of *the Express* at Cologne airport.

In my running report for the early edition - followed rapidly by a re-write and a final local emphasis report - I questioned Liverpool's tactics.

Shanks was livid, though I suspect I had hit a small nail on the head. Perhaps the nail was not so small. In Cologne airport the players were amused at my public rollicking by Shanks. They shuffled uneasily in the background. Soon, as was his nature, it became clear that Shanks had moved on to other matters and I was off the hook, so Ian St. John, a hugely talented player and a likeable and impish man, took the chance to chortle in Shankly's hearing that he had directed me to the ladies room instead of the men's. Shanks enjoyed that pointed riposte at my expense and I liked my snappy response to St. John even more, as I returned to the party. "I'm the first guy you've sent the wrong way all season," it was a rare shaft of lacerating wit.

Oddly enough, another barb of unexpected and pleasing sharpness was unleashed on Tommy Smith on another occasion. I met the powerhouse Liverpool captain as he strolled along the corridor of a Manchester hotel in the team's pre-match headquarters.

"Still writing crap?" he taunted as he walked by after a formal greeting.

"Yes," I replied and with a speed of response that pleased me and with quickening pace to widen our distance, I rapped back over my shoulder: "Are you still playing it?"

Smith rarely fell below a high standard of rugged excellence and besides being a gruff humorist, he had an artistic touch as demonstrated after Liverpool swamped

Borussia Moenchengladbach 3-1 in Rome at the beginning of a six year run of triumphs for English teams in the European Cup from 1977 to 1982. After Borrusia, Liverpool beat Bruges at Wembley to be followed by Nottingham Forest (twice). Liverpool then beat Real Madrid in Paris in 1981, with Aston Villa rounding off the six hit.

THE ROAD TO ROME AND BEYOND

FIVE DAYS HAD seemed hardly long enough for Liverpool to cast aside the disappointment of a treble-busting 2-1 defeat by Manchester United in the 1977 F.A. Cup Final and re-charge mental and physical batteries for the test against Borussia Moenchengladbach on the European stage in Rome. More than 25,000 supporters took the road to the Italian capital where Paisley made one change from the team beaten by United at Wembley, Ian Callaghan replacing David "Super Sub" Johnson.

Smith scored a vital goal in his 600th game in a red shirt with a powerful header to turn the game around after Dane Allan Simonsen finally beat the outstandingly competent Ray Clemence to equalise a goal by Terry McDermott supplied by the brilliance of Steve Heighway. Phil Neal's perfect penalty was the grim footnote for the beaten Germans.

Smith demonstrated his artistic side when he spotted an easel supporting a paper-covered notice board, probably used for tactical illustrations, as the squad waited in the corridors of the stadium for their transport back to the hotel and the inevitable and prolonged celebration. On it Smith drew, with considerable artistic flair, a mighty caricature of himself leaping high to head a superb goal from a corner by Heighway with goalkeeper Wolfgang Kneib represented as a timorous mouse. "Can't stand mice," smiled Smith. "They frighten me." Rivals never frightened Smith who chose Rome to score for the club he had joined at 14.

It was a night Kevin Keegan never forgot. Keegan plagued the hugely talented Berti Vogts – the same likeable Berti who failed as manager of Scotland - from start to finish in his farewell appearance before he moved on to Hamburg in a half a million pound deal. "Nothing can compare with this" beamed Bob Paisley, the first English-born manager to lift the European Cup.

Bob Paisley turned Liverpool into defensive misers of the English game, combining the skill to strike with devastating speed in the spectacular Seventies when the decade yielded championship successes in 1973, 1976, 1977,1979 and 1980 with runners-up spots claimed in 1974, 1975, 1978. The convincing success of 1979, eight points clear of Nottingham Forest, was a season of record breaking defensive excellence and a stark example of how a strong defensive foundation is a pre-requisite to the building of a successful team; an obvious basic ignored by so many although there have been isolated examples of a brilliant attack carrying a modest defence.

Liverpool conceded only 16 goals in a 42-game campaign (or .38 of goal a game) a record that stood until 2005 when Chelsea conceded only 15 goals (though in a 38-game season) slipstreaming Arsenal by 12 points and third-placed Manchester United by an incredible 18. It is significant how few defensive changes

Liverpool and Chelsea were obliged to make in their statements of solidarity. Goalkeeper Ray Clemence and right back Phil Neal played all 42 games in 1978-79, left back Ray Kennedy missed only five and centre backs Phil Thompson (39) and Alan Hansen (34) were never missing for long spells.

Notwithstanding Jose Mourinho's reputation for making unforced changes, goalkeeper Petr Cech missed only three of the 38 games in 2004-5, but the attendance figures are less impressive than Liverpool's record sequence. Right back Paulo Ferreira played 29 times, one more than left back William Gallas and the amazingly consistent John Terry missed just two games with his partner Ricardo Carvalho playing 22 plus three as a substitute. Liverpool manager Rafa Benitez made the hardly surprising discovery late in 2005 that "if you don't concede goals and have good players further forward, you are going to win a lot of games." He then added the starkly obvious: "I know the great Liverpool teams from the past based their success along those lines and it is the only way." Quite so!

It is worth recalling that Real Madrid won the trophy for the first five years of its existence, topped by the breathtaking 7-3 defeat of Eintracht Frankfurt in Glasgow, arguably the most engaging game in the history of soccer. Liverpool's comeback against AC Milan in Istanbul from three goals down was breathtaking. Manchester United's triumph at the Nou Camp in 1999 was schoolboy comic stuff; truth stranger than football fiction.

The 'puppet-on-a-string' gamesmanship employed

by Bruce Grobbelaar in a shoot-out when Liverpool returned to Rome in 1984 to crush Roma 4-2 on penalties after a 1-1 draw, did not infringe the laws or the spirit of the game. The ploy was repeated in the final of 2005 when Jerzy Dudek successfully reproduced the distracting tactics of his extrovert predecessor. The game was a nostalgic reminder of the skill from the penalty spot of Charlie Mitten of Manchester United. I once checked with the left wing legend that he had never missed a penalty kick. "Yes, I did once," he said. "But I scored from the deflected rebound."

Surely no scriptwriter could improve the story of the final in 2005. Not only did Liverpool recover from 3-0 down at half time, a somewhat flattering scoreline to AC Milan, they triumphed in arguably the most dramatic match about-turn and penalty shoot-out of all time. The live drama in Istanbul tended to obscure the statistical significance of Liverpool's fifth success in the tournament, won three times under the command of Bob Paisley and once when managed by Joe Fagan, formerly a Manchester City player. What was not generally realised was that Liverpool's success shot England to the top of the European soccer league with a bag of 28 trophies ending the domination of Spain and Italy with 27.

Then for the romantics and perhaps the day-dream punters there were omens galore about the success at a stadium built to support Turkey's bid for the Olympics swirling round Liverpool's successes of 1978 and 1981. In 1978 and 2005, the Welsh won the Grand Slam, the Pope passed on and the League Cup winners also drove on to win the League Championship. The years of 1981 when Liverpool beat Real Madrid 1-0 in Paris and 2005 had milestone happenings outside the world of soccer. Prince Charles married, Ken and Deidre made it to the altar to the delight of Coronation Street fans and a new Dr. Who made his bow. Those with a fascination for colour will have noted that Liverpool's four previous successes were gained in red shirts against teams in white (Borussia, FC Bruges, Real Madrid and Roma). AC Milan had their red shirts lined up with Liverpool in their change strip. But AC with a touch of superstition Liverpool would understand, the Italians were happy to make a switch and parade in their white away strip they wore when winning the trophy in 1989, 1990, 1994 and 2003.

It was the comeback of comebacks in Europe's major tournament, outstripping even the feat of Real Madrid in the first tournament in 1956 when the Spanish heroes recovered from two goals down in just ten minutes to beat Reims 4-3. However, it was impossible not to feel sorry for Hernan Crespo, later to return to Chelsea, who was the first player to score twice and finish on the losing team since Real's Ferenc Puskas grabbed a hat-trick in 1962 when Benfica triumphed 5-3 in Amsterdam.

Such fascinating stats and quirks had no part in the throbbing brains and pulsating hearts of the players and the 65,000 spectators who struggled to even locate and then gain admission to the "outback" stadium. Even the most optimistic Liverpool supporter must have felt there was a hollow ring to their brave chants when 3-0 down at half-time "we're gonna win 4-3." You could see in the faces of the 40,000 who had paid fortunes to be there, that it would take all their urging and more to heave Liverpool out of their despair as they had done on a lesser scale against Chelsea in the semi-final. The Liverpool manager Rafael Benitez must have spoken magic words at half-time; surely not so inspirational as to conjure three goals in six minutes of the second half by Gerrard, Smicer and Xabi Alonso to bring hundreds of fans back from the threshold of the exit gates.

The subsequent shoot-out made compelling viewing for the TV cameras: Serginho missed, Hamann 0-1, Pirlo saved, Cisse 0-2, Tomasson 1-2, Riise saved, Kaka 2-2, Smicer 2-3, Shevchenko saved. Dudek could have plaited sawdust as they say in Knotty Ash. Many who didn't before, now believed in fairies. And Liverpool kept the cup for good.

★

The swashbuckling success in Turkey was in stark contrast to the beginning of Liverpool's European trail in the late summer of 1964 with a first round tie against the part-timers of KR Reykjavik in Iceland. We queued at immigration at Reykjavik airport after landing between small prefab buildings then surrounding the runway. Suddenly a young Icelandic man struggled past Shankly clutching a package of tea chest proportions. "Move over there boys," Shanks ordered his players, "there's a boy coming through with his hoose." Shankly had evidently not failed to observe the tiny wooden huts and his wisecrack was perfection.

Earlier on the flight from Glasgow, two colleagues, their work for the day complete, had been reluctant to ignore the cabin attendant's hospitality with the drinks trolley. As we approached Reykjavik at dusk, the pilot swooped low over the smouldering island volcano, Sertse. Just to ensure that we had marvelled at the pink glow in the sea on the starboard side, the pilot, still regaling his passengers with volcanic folklore over the intercom, turned round and swooped back again with Sertse on the port side this time. The man from *The Sun* learned across to view the spectacle and pronounced: "Look at the sea… its full of flipping volcanoes."

But even Shankly had been rendered speechless earlier in the journey. With time to kill before leaving Scottish soil, Shanks ordered the coach driver to whisk the squad on a time-occupying tour. He hailed the gateman at the local holiday camp expecting the gates to be flung open in welcome for a tour of the grounds with the words "We are Liverpool football club – we're on our way to Iceland."

"Aye, that's as may be – but you're way off course," replied the loyal custodian of the camp. The barrier stayed down. But Liverpool's progress on the field of play was inevitable with two goals each from Roger Hunt and Gordon Wallace with Phil Chisnall scoring the fifth to conclude the tie. Even so, 32,500 turned out at Anfield for the second leg to watch a game their team could hardly lose.

Shankly staunchly believed that players only became injured when they lost their concentration. Those who were in the treatment room were ignored and not considered to be part of the squad until they were fully fit again. Yet Shanks lost his concentration on one memorable occasion in Bucharest. Peter Robinson, the club's loyal secretary and Jim Kennefick, an executive of Aer Lingus who had flown Liverpool deep behind the Iron Curtain, found themselves on the touchline sitting near Shanks instead of in the stand. Alun Evans was injured and the deeply engrossed Shanks mumbled to the bench about his replacement. Without thinking, Kennefick muttered "Phil Boersema" who was sitting next to him. "You're on, son," rapped Shankly still immersed in the action. It turned out to be a successful, if unorthodox, substitution.

THE PAISLEY/FAGAN MACHINE

WHEN BILL SHANKLY suddenly announced he was to quit football in the summer of 1974 it stunned Merseyside. Shanks ignored the pleadings of then chairman John Smith and the club secretary Peter Robinson. "We went down on our bended knees to try and persuade Bill to change his mind," recalled Robinson. Bob Paisley, content as a highly valued assistant, also tried to influence Shanks into a change of mind. "I suggested Bill have a break and then come back," Paisley said but to no avail.

So Bob took over at the age of 55 when most men are thinking about armchairs and slippers. "I reasoned that if I accepted the job it would prevent the whole backroom staff being disturbed. I looked upon myself as a buffer until they got a new manager and I told the players that." Some buffer! When Paisley retired nine seasons later his successes included three European Cups, six League championships, three League Cups, one UEFA Cup and one European Super Cup.

Ian Callaghan, a player with an incredible 'engine' and a consistent performer across two decades, was the only first team player to span Shankly's reign from the old Second Division to the 1977 triumph in the European Cup. He made an apt summing up: "Shanks was the greatest motivator in the world. But Bob was the finest tactician." Ian could have added that Bob was also the most modest and humble of men who could deliver a comprehensive tactical breakdown on a team with a ten minute viewing. And I never saw him take a note, unlike some of his predecessors who seem unable to take charge without notebooks and tape recorders.

Paisley's career had not been all sweetness and success. World War Two quickly followed his arrival at Anfield from Bishop Auckland in 1939 and after 277 games his career arrived at a crossroads. Having retired from playing he joined the backroom staff in 1954. One career crunch for Paisley came when he was left out of the 1950 F.A. Cup Final team (Arsenal won 2-0) and was persuaded to stay at Anfield by his close friend and team-mate Albert Stubbins. A second career crunch for the resilient and patient Paisley came when Shankly arrived in December, 1959.

Shanks 'culled' 24 players from his inherited staff, but rather than recruit his own backroom team, he kept the training staff, including Bob the builder (well bricklayer) who learned physiotherapy from a correspondence course and by observing procedures at local hospitals.

Paisley's first signing was the 'unknown' Phil Neal (50 England caps) from Northampton. Other signings from obscurity included Ian Rush (73 outings for Wales), Alan Hansen (26 for Scotland), Steve Nicol (27 for Scotland) and goalkeeper Bruce Grobbelaar also capped by Zimbabwe and remembered for his eccentricity as well as his skill between the sticks. Other notable Paisley signings: Kenny Dalglish, Graeme Souness, and Mark Lawrenson figured with outstanding success in the club and international arena while the conversion of Ray Kennedy, signed from Arsenal in 1974 for a modest £180,000, from striker to the left side of mid-field, was a masterstroke for team and player.

Paisley had a "chuckly" sense of humour and enjoyed a prank. One such jape was definitely not PC. Before he took over from Shanks, he sat in the middle of the team coach on its way through Milan after a game, his hair brushed down in the shape of a Hitler hair-do with part of a black comb under his nose to represent a moustache.

Among his chief attributes was the ability to speak sparingly but make every word count. Paisley was at his best after the 1977 triumph in Rome against Borussia Moenchengladbach in the first of five European Cup success for Liverpool in six Finals. Rome was alight with Liverpool glee. The Holiday Inn St. Peter's was the setting for the after-match celebrations of the management, squad, directors and media. It was a bedlam of alcoholic joy. Bob stood at the bar. "I think the Pope and I are the only two people in Rome sober tonight," he smiled. "I like a drink, but tonight I'm drinking in the occasion. I want to savour every marvellous moment of this." He could not resist the ps: "The last time I was in Rome was in 1944 when I drove in a tank."

The Paisley era was the meat between Bill Shankly and Joe Fagan in an amazing Liverpool sandwich unsurpassed for its power and consistency. Fagan was as reluctant as Paisley to forsake a role as supernumary to take over the managerial reins at Anfield at the age of 62, just two years younger than Bob who had retired. In his first season, Liverpool became the first English side to net three major trophies in a season. "Fabulous" Fagan, a rugged centre half with Manchester City and Bradford PA, led his team to title success in 1984, three points ahead of Southampton, to become the first team since Arsenal in the 30s to win three successive titles. It had been a slog of a season for Liverpool. Yet only 16 players were employed – Gary Gillespie signed by Joe on his first day in charge played only once – in a gruelling 66 games in nine months representing almost two games a week.

Ian Rush was voted Player of the Year by his PFA colleagues and by the Football Writers' Association and also scooped the Golden Boot as Europe's top marksman with 48 goals in 64 games plus 32 in 41 League matches, including five against Luton Town, four against Coventry City and a hat-trick at Aston Villa. Rushie also shattered Roger Hunt's record haul in a season of 42 strikes in all matches and 30 goals in the League.

It was not surprising, therefore, that Rush hit his club century with a flourish (two against Dinamo Bucharest in the European Cup semi-final second leg) akin to a batsman reaching his ton with a six over square leg. The stat of 100 goals in 166 matches – underlines the power and pace of the Welshman who was born just a few miles from England.

It was bound to be a tension-packed match against AS Roma in Rome; an expectation that was fulfilled with goals by Phil Neal and Roberto Pruzzo being the prelude to a penalty shoot-out. Steve Nicol fired over the bar before successful kicks by Neal, Souness and Rush (naturally) led up to Grobbelaar's 'spaghetti legs' antics that presumably induced Francesco Graziani to miscue his shot into the Roman sky. It was Alan Kennedy against Franco Tancredi for the title. Franco dived expecting "Barney" to shoot as usual to the 'keeper's left. Kennedy's shot zoomed to the other side and Souness lifted the Cup in his last game for Liverpool before moving to Sampdoria in Italy. Fagan later signed John Wark from Ipswich who switched the goals emphasis with 27 in his first season, but Evertonians had their revenge for being part of the hat-trick the previous season by clinching their third title since the war with a mighty 13 points to spare over Liverpool, the runners-up.

No Evertonian could have enjoyed the subsequent grim climax to Fagan's managership. Liverpool had raised doubts about the suitability of the Heysel Stadium in Brussels some time before the final against Juventus when success would have given Liverpool the trophy in celebration of five successes, a feat delayed until 2005. In a sad shambles, security and ticket checks were inadequate and Juventus fans infiltrated one section of the Liverpool end that had been declared a "neutral" area. A hot atmosphere became even hotter and a group of Liverpool fans charged a flimsy fence and a wall collapsed causing 39 deaths and many injuries. Liverpool lost much more than the final to a penalty by the magical Michel Platini that night and Fagan returned home a sad and devastated man and into retirement.

It is worth remembering that Everton had kick-started the Merseyside success rollercoaster in winning the First Division title in the freeze-up, knees-up, season of 1962-63. Liverpool said "snap" the following season and totalled 13 success in 27 years before the Premier League was formed in 1992. Manchester United then went on a rampage equalling Liverpool's three in a row in 1999, 2000, and 2001 and winning eight of the first 11 PL titles. The success bandwagon had a fascinating undertone.

Shankly had a fanatic's regard for Bobby Charlton, so much so that when Liverpool stayed at their overnight HQ in Lymm near Manchester, he would visit Bobby, who lived nearby, for a cup of his favourite beverage, tea. It was not until many years later that Charlton realised the meetings could easily have been construed as an 'illegal approach' of Chelsea dimensions. "I thought highly of Bill, of course, but I often wondered afterwards if his visits were more than social," Charlton recalled. "His enthusiasm was electrifying if not even a shade terrifying."

Not many won an argument or debate with Shanks although I once won a bet and it concerned Charlton. Shanks was drooling about Bobby's skills down the left flank for club and country, reflecting on the power of Charlton's left foot which Shanks insisted was his natural side. I pointed out that Bobby was naturally a right-footed player. Bill was unconvinced until I asked him which foot Bobby took a penalty kick with. "Jeese, son, you're right – his right," admitted Shanks.

Emlyn 'Crazy Horse' Hughes, a key figure in Liverpool's success, once recalled a game at Anfield where George Best had destroyed Liverpool almost single-handedly. The players gathered in silence for the anticipated Shankly rollicking afterwards. Eventually he arrived in the dressing room, stood in his Jimmy Cagney stance hands on hips and proclaimed: "Boys, you've just been beaten by a genius," and strode out of the hushed dressing room.

The bond between Hughes and Shankly, like so many other of his players, was touchingly loyal. Mind you, Shanks and Emlyn got off on the right boot, so to speak. Knowing that Emlyn had a competitor's heritage through his father who played Rugby League, Shankly knew he had struck gold when he signed Hughes from Blackpool. Driving on the way to register the signing at the Football League's HQ at nearby St. Annes, Shankly was stopped for speeding in his haste to complete the deal. Shankly stifled the "hello, hello, hello" approach of the speedcop by announcing: "This is Emlyn Hughes, a future captain of England. He's just signed for Liverpool and we're on our way to St. Annes to complete the signing." A stunned PC recognised Shankly and waved the car on. Once again, Shanks was proved right.

TALKING BOOTS

JOE FAGAN'S successor, Kenny Dalglish, was not always easy to understand with his guttural Scots accent and low-decibel delivery. He let his boots do the talking and masterminded a hat-trick of titles at the helm of Liverpool (1985-6, 1987-8, 1989-90) before adding to his impressive collection of medals by inspiring Blackburn Rovers to the championship in 1994-5.

Managers to have won the F.A. Cup with different clubs include Billy Walker who won it with Sheffield Wednesday in 1935 and Nottingham Forest in 1959. Herbert Chapman led Huddersfield Town to Cup success in 1922 and did a repeat in charge of Arsenal in 1930. Yet such deeds were outshone by Kenny Dalglish and George Graham (Arsenal) who achieved the Championship/F.A. Cup double as both player and manager with a single club. Joe Mercer went one better winning the Championship as a player with Everton, the title twice and the F.A. Cup once as a player with Arsenal and then won both competitions as manager of Manchester City aided and abetted by Malcolm Allison.

Mark Hughes seemed to make a habit of winning F.A. Cup medals – three for Manchester United, one for Chelsea.

Yet many players of star status were never winners in the great soccer lottery. They include such giants as Tommy Lawton, Tom Finney, Johnny Haynes, Gordon Banks, George Best, Terry Butcher, Peter Shilton, Martin Peters, Nobby Stiles, Alan Ball and Malcolm Macdonald. Right winger Jimmy Delaney, first signing by Sir Matt

Busby for Manchester United, had a unique collection of gongs in English, Northern Ireland and Republic of Ireland football. He hit the jackpot with Celtic (1937), Manchester United (1948), and Derry City (1954) and was a runner-up with Cork City two years later. Manchester United always seem to claim unusual niches in cup football... Martin Buchan was the first player to skipper Scottish and English F.A. Cup-winning teams with Aberdeen in 1970 and Manchester United against Liverpool in 1977.

JOVIAL JOE

JOE MERCER, of the famed England half-back line of Britton, Cullis and Mercer, could match any manager for tactical know-how and he had a wicked sense of humour. Mercer took Malcolm Allison from Plymouth to help him re-build Manchester City, gave him a free hand on training and tactics and stood by him to the end after doubts about Malcolm's loyalty when the axe, politically wielded, cruelly and improperly fell on Joe at Maine Road.

They were football's Morecambe and Wise in that each understood the other's thoughts although the comic/straight-man roles were frequently reversed. Allison was an inventive and hard-working coach, toiling endlessly to improve player fitness and skills. Allison would spend hours after training banging shots to the 'weak' left side of goalkeeper Joe Corrigan. Without the VIP treatment, Corrigan would never have been such a successful and commanding goalkeeping giant in every sense, though legend always had it that despite being well over six feet tall, he was the midget in the family from Sale. Joe gave Malcolm licence to thrill by backing his up-dated coaching methods as their relationship developed to the advantage of Manchester City.

Malcolm was always eccentric; once he departed from home one Friday evening on a mission to buy fish and chips and did not return until the following Tuesday, so the unchallenged legend maintained. Fascinating and revealing in-depth Allison columns were ghosted by James Lawton in the *Daily Express*.

Francis Lee joined the ranks of locally recruited youngsters like Neil Young, Alan Oakes, his cousin Glyn Pardoe, Tommy Booth, Nicky Reid, Paul Power (literally a lawyer rather than the dressing room lawyer) and Colin Bell, whose energy was such that the players called him Nijinsky after the Derby-Oaks-St. Leger winning racehorse.

Mercer asked his chief scout Harry Godwin: "Is Bell ready for us yet?" Two words, "Yes, boss," was all Joe needed to do a deal with Bury. Bob Paisley was in the stands when Bell was seriously injured playing against Manchester United. "That lad's got a bad knee – he'll struggle to ever play again at this level," Paisley confided afterwards in a remarkably accurate diagnosis from a seat in the stands.

A record signing at £45,000, Bell was a key figure in the team that won the League title, heading United by two points in 1968, only for United to trump that feat by winning their first European crown a few weeks later. Bell's total of almost 500 senior games included the Cup Winners' Cup success and victory in the League Cup.

Few players have been blessed with a more powerful football 'engine' than Bell. He had a sprinter's pace, a middle-distance runner's stamina and the heart of a marathon man. Players such as Peter Doherty, Emlyn Hughes, Colin Harvey, Steve Gerrard, Roy Keane, Bryan Robson and Dave Mackay, are among those who challenge Bell for sheer athletic ability.

Yet one tackle wrecked that flourishing career at the age of 29 with Bell set to rack up 750 games or more for City and possibly doubling the 48 England caps he had earned by the time a challenge by Manchester United captain Martin Buchan in November 1975 left Bell's right knee and upper shin a twisted mess. For those with a close view from the Press box, it was a stark reminder of the pain and consequences of a sudden unexpected career-ending indicent. Yes, players earn big money, but a moment's misfortune can shatter even the greatest of careers.

For almost four years, Bell, a quiet and withdrawn man unlike so many of his team-mates, fought a brave and lonely battle to recover from that horrific clash. "It felt like my leg had been screwed into the ground," Bell recalled in his biography, "Reluctant Hero" published forty years after the event. "My leg bent backwards, bursting blood vessels in the bottom of my thigh and in the top of my calf. All the ligaments in my knee were torn. Within seconds the knee was just a bag of blood. My knee had swollen to the size of a football and my leg was black and blue. And I was generally unwell, too. I was told by a doctor that the trauma was similar to that suffered by someone involved in a serious road smash."

If the signing of Bell had been a formality, the capture of Tony Book by Allison was unorthodox, and surely inspirational. Book had been at Plymouth with Allison, and sampled non-League combat with Bath City where he was part-time right back, part-time bricklayer. A few eyebrows were raised when Book arrived at Maine Road – aged 29! - where he laid the foundations of an exceptional career, leading by example as an energetic right-back and captain who rarely dropped bricks on the pitch. The signing of Dennis Tueart from Sunderland was another masterstroke. Who could forget his overhead goal against Newcastle United in the League Cup Final of 1976?

Yet not all Malcolm's signings proved as fruitful. Allison's urge to sign Rodney Marsh from QPR was understandable. He fitted City's quest for unpredictable talent with individuality and flair and a dash of the outrageous. Unfortunately, instead of soaring up the table and strengthening a challenge for the title, City faded out of the scene after his arrival. Marsh, however, was a much-appreciated cavalier who charmed and frustrated the Maine Road public and won eight caps in the process. The prelude to Marsh's arrival in March 1972 was personally unusual to say the least. A teatime call from a friend of executive rank at British Airways and a football zealot and player of town team quality in his youth, went thus: "City have just booked a flight from Manchester to Heathrow for Eric Alexander (the City chairman). What's that all about?"

"They're going to sign Rodney Marsh," I replied. "Book me on the flight." Roger Charlesworth did and promised to bend the rules by delaying the flight for ten minutes. I dashed from The Express Building in Manchester, changed in my pal's office – and took my seat. Once airborne, I sent a note via a member of the cabin crew to Eric Alexander, the chairman of Manchester City, twenty rows up the aircraft to let him know the *Daily Express* was on his tail. His upraised hand movement without turning his head was less personal and insulting than the passengers behind him may have thought!

We shared a taxi to the West End. The Marsh deal was done and *The Express* netted the exclusive. Eric was to later remind me of my comment about Marsh, who I found to be charming and humorous as well as a gifted and outrageous footballer. "Rodney won't be happy until he's headed a goal from the penalty spot," I once remarked to Alexander. He knew what I meant. We also knew what Eric's father Albert Alexander meant when he said during his reign as chairman after City's success in the First Division title race of 1967-8: "Now we're in Europe we can afford to go out and buy some good players."

City ultimately made a disastrous decision to dispense with the services of Uncle Joe, everybody's favourite. Rather than retaining him in some image-spinning exercise, they literally sent him to Coventry. Some time before he recruited Gordon Milne, the cultured wing half who missed Liverpool's F.A. Cup jinx-breaking win against Leeds United in 1965, Manchester City were visited Highfield Road. There was never a doubt that Joe would jovially greet the visiting hierarchy, long since forgetting the pain he had felt at his departure from Maine Road. As he mingled in the entrance hall, Joe was chatting animatedly to the visiting directors and officials when he suddenly looked at his watch.

"Good heavens, look at the time" he exclaimed, "it's a quarter to three – I'd better get down to the dressing room and confuse them a bit more."

Such was Joe's character that Mike Summerbee instigated his departure from Swindon Town to Manchester City by telephoning the manager and offering his services. Summerbee, out-going off the field as well as on it, always claimed that he was "the only player to tap a manager." Once I ventured to suggest to Asa Hartford, then enduring a miserable time at Everton, that he should ring John Bond. I made it easy for Hartford by slipping him the number of Bond's home in Mere. A deal went through soon afterwards and Hartford spent many years at Maine Road in several important roles after his playing career ended.

Like Bryan Robson and many others, Mercer had a disregard for the consequence of injuries during his playing days. There was a memorable picture of the day when he was carried off on a stretcher at Highbury with his arm raised in a wave of farewell, acknowledging that at nearing 40 his playing days were over, ended by a broken leg playing for the club he joined from Everton in 1946. "I nearly made it back and played again," he confided later, conveniently overlooking the bone structure of his legs that would not successfully stop a dog in an entry.

OLD TIME TRICKS

LONG BEFORE the advent of football's transfer window, football retained more than a measure of intrigue and deception. One intriguing example was the unusual and deception-shrouded arrival at Old Trafford from Barnsley in 1953 of Tommy Taylor who led England's attack 19 times before his death at Munich. Surely no transfer before or since cold have involved more intrigue and cunning.

Busby's aide Jimmy Murphy had filed glowing assessments. Matt went to watch Taylor himself against Birmingham. "I knew he was the boy to complete my pattern," Busby concluded, leaving the game after half an hour to minimise the significance of his visit, knowing other clubs were keenly interested in Taylor.

After taking refuge in a pub near Barnsley for two days and ensuring they escaped the notice of rival bidders, the pair emerged to make a firm offer Barnsley could hardly refuse. Barnsley demanded the astronomical fee of £30,000 for Taylor – United paid one pound less. "I didn't want the lad tagged a thirty thousand pound player," reasoned Busby. "It was such a big label to bear." He handed the spare quid to the char lady who had kept the tea flowing throughout the fraught negotiations.

Ferguson's spending sprees (later eclipsed by Chelsea) dwarfed Busby's wheeling and dealing. Ferguson is a complex man, immensely proud of his roots in Govan with a political view definitely left of centre. Yet he rightly sees nothing illogical in donning morning dress and mingling with aristocratic Ascot crowds many of whom might be more likely to know the ins and outs of fetlock and furlongs than footballers and the pedigree of the man who drove United to eight League titles, five F.A. Cups, the European Cup, Cup Winners Cup, League Cup and Inter-Continental Cup by 2005. He swept into Old Trafford; a new broom – with a wise (and prickly) head determined to fill the 25 year void left by his Scottish predecessor, Sir Matt.

FERGIE AT THE CROSS ROADS.

UNTIL ONE of the principals involved violates a pledge of silence and secrecy (or Sir Alex himself admits it) we shall never know how close Fergie came to taking over as the first non-Englishman to become supremo at Lancaster Gate. Research at the time and subsequently encourage a strong view: *very close*. Sir Alex had been informally invited several years before to give his views on international managership in general and in particular the candidates who might be of England managerial material. Sir Alex was quizzed about the merits of his stalwart Manchester United captain Bryan Robson, Kevin Keegan, Gerry Francis (who it seemed always had the potential to be a top manager), Howard Kendall and a few others. Fergie was never informally short-listed or even given the most obscure hint. Until, that is, when Terry Venables kept his promise and quit at the end of season 1994-96. As they do on these occasions, the F.A. formed a sub-committee comprising of Graham Kelly (former chief of the Football League and F.A.), Bert Millichip, Keith Wiseman, Chris Willcox (F.A. vice chairman), Noel White (chairman of the senior international committee) and the former distinguished England captain and club manager Jimmy Armfield. The F.A. made a formal approach to the Manchester United board whose reaction was to re-new Fergie's contract that only had another year to run.

"I had the distinct impression that Fergie might be interested," Armfield cautiously recalled in his autobiography, "Right Back to the Beginning." Later Sir Alex admitted he would have "liked the chance to talk a bit more." In the event Glenn Hoddle succeeded Venables and reigned until his ill advised book about the 1998 World Cup and a less than friendly media ended his tenure in February 1999 rather than his record as a coach. Howard Wilkinson (caretaker), Kevin Keegan, and Peter Taylor (caretaker) were in charge for some two years and three months until a non-Englishman, Sven-Goran Eriksson, *was* appointed.

It is interesting to speculate on what might have been at Manchester United and England had Fergie taken the helm his predecessors had held so uncertainly. In another fascinating twist of managerial fate, many Mancunians believe that Sir Alex changed his decision to retire when he discovered what United were to pay Sven-Goran Eriksson as his possible successor. Another intriguing chapter for the Ferguson memoirs.

Ferguson, of course, had experienced management at international level when he took over after Jock Stein died in 1985. It was not a particularly happy time for the widely experienced apprentice who became such a successful sorcerer. But Fergie was at the crossroads after fronting Scotland's campaign in Mexico following

Stein's sudden death during the qualifying run-in. He ultimately decided against taking charge of Scotland permanently and also turned down offers of work in several prominent English League clubs.

It was the first time there had been a hint even of defection by the son of a shipyard worker born in Govan, Glasgow, on New Year's Eve 1941. Sir Alex learned the game through the ranks of Govan High School, Glasgow Schools and Scotland Youth and for his country as an amateur. Before joining Queen's Park in 1957, Fergie was associated with two of Scotland's most famous junior clubs, Harmony Row BC and Drumchapel Amateurs. Stranraer in the Second Division was his first taste of the Scottish League before a move took him to St.Johnstone and later Dunfermline Athletic in 1964 as a full time pro.

His next stop was Rangers in 1967 where he spent two and a half years before joining Falkirk where he sampled management for the first time. Then there followed a part time reign at Ayr United in September 1973 coupled with running his public house, Fergie's Bar in Glasgow. The nomad's caravan was still rolling... manager of East Stirling in July 1974 and three months later he took over at St. Mirren, leading them to the Second Division title in his first full season. Aberdeen was the next port of call in 1978 where a career that had been quietly flourishing suddenly burst into life.

Under the Ferguson baton, the Dons won three Premier League titles, the Scottish Cup four times, the League Cup once and the European Cup Winners' Cup. It was the biggest trawl of trophies in Aberdeen's history.

Such spectacular success earned Fergie an OBE and a seat on the Pittodrie Board of Directors. Offers, formal and informal, of work in England flowed in after his stint with the national team ended until the ultimate challenge came from Manchester United to succeed Ron Atkinson who had done so much to revitalise Old Trafford.

Not even the most optimistic minded Fergie, nor the board that appointed him, could have expected such a spectacular explosion after he survived an uncertain three-year spell following his long-delayed move south in November, 1986. Charisma was combined with ruthless objectivity; power allied to the softest of touches. His professionalism and devotion was absolute. He would rage at what he considered to be an injustice and yet he could put a comforting arm round the shoulders of any player down on his luck. He could treat the media disgracefully or regally, yet he could always 'spin' with a political flourish to further the interests of the club or himself. He had an editor's knowledge of what makes news. Success, of course, is the best news of all.

The honours sideboard was crammed in 15 and a half years of spectacular and unprecedented glory. A CBE in the 1995 New Year's Honours' list was followed by a Knighthood for his services to football four years later. Sir Alex became the first manager to lead a club to three successive English championships in 2001 (and repeated the feat 8 years later - Ed). Even Fergie could not match the successeses of four managers who won the English League championship with different clubs. Tom Watson did it with Sunderland and Liverpool before Herbert

Chapman took Huddersfield Town to the title in 1923-4 and 1924-5, later moving south to steer Arsenal to the title in 1930-31 and 1932-33. Brian Clough joined the elite, taking the helm at Derby County in 1971-72 before boosting Nottingham Forest's image in 1977-8. Although he remains the only manager to win both the Scottish and English leagues.

JACK'S LUCK OF THE IRISH

The Republic and Northern Ireland shared the knack of grabbing centre stage at the expense of England, Scotland or Wales. The Republic knew how to celebrate success alright and the party included the nation's President. When Ireland shook the English and set the 1988 European Championship finals alight with a 1-0 victory in Stuttgart, John Bean and I were in Jack Charlton's suite revelling in the *craic* when the telephone rang.

"It's the President for you, Jack," said his assistant Mick Byrne. "It can wait," replied Jack, "I'm busy," and replaced the telephone, presuming the call had come from the President Hotel in Dublin where his team had stayed. The call came through again.

"No," insisted Byrne, "it's THE President...the President of Ireland who wants to speak to YOU." "Jeeses," said Big Jack after a long silence, "what do I call him? 'Mr. President' I presume."

The winning goal was scored by Ray Houghton who six years later was to repeat his scoring prowess to give the Republic a 1-0 win against Italy before a crowd of 80,000 in the Giants Stadium, New York. Victory over England was followed by a 1-1 draw with the USSR in

Hanover, Ronnie Whelan scoring with a 30-yard left foot volley he never surpassed for its brilliance and few players have equalled for the perfection of its execution. A 1-0 defeat by Holland, then at the peak of an impressive spell of controlled and sedate football under the guidance of players of the calibre of Ruud Gullitt, Marco Van Basten, and Ronald Koeman. It was Koeman who unhinged a brave Irish performance when his header looked to be going wide of goal until substitute Wym Kieft scored with a desperately lucky lunge.

Ireland returned home to Dublin the following day to be greeted by a crowd of almost 200,000 who roared their appreciation of an impressive team tactically and individually. It always seemed that Charlton and his entourage were able to make a better job of scaling big mountains with the motto 'the impossible we do at once; miracles take a little longer'.

Billy Bingham, you sensed, looked for and found mobility and fire to make up for any inadequacies, whereas the swashbuckling team under Peter Doherty that had reached the quarter-finals in Sweden in 1958 had quality in depth. It always seemed that the North of Ireland and the Republic could always find a missing magical quality exactly when it was needed most.

Until Big Jack's arrival, the Republic of Ireland seemed to be expert at snatching defeat from the jaws of victory. Managers had come and gone in unspectacular procession until Eoin Hand's departure at the end of 1985 following a disappointing World Cup qualifying campaign (climaxed by a 4-1 defeat at home to Denmark) brought the FAI to a crossroads and, after many bouts of political in-fighting, ultimately to its senses. The Republic always seems to have great players over the years (John Carey, Charlie Hurley, and Johnny Giles) without ever qualifying for a major tournament until Big Jack took over. In the mid-eighties, the squad looked stronger and more promising than ever with stars like Mark Lawrenson, Liam Brady, Frank Stapleton, Kevin Moran, David O'Leary and Ronnie Whelan on the scene, yet as a team the stars failed to gel.

After Hand's departure, Manchester City refused to release Billy McNeil. There was much skulduggery behind the confused scenes and even a move to persuade Bob Paisley to take over in Dublin where over the years interest in soccer had been diluted by passions for sports of special appeal to the Irish. Others interviewed included Johnny Giles, who had managed Ireland between 1973 and 1980, Noel Cantwell, Terry Neill, formerly manager of Arsenal, Gordon Lee and Paddy Crerand who had a fan's respect for the Irish but had little experience of management.

Eventually in February 1986 Charlton was appointed, not, it must be said, with unanimous approval. Many Irish fans wanted Liam Tuohy. The Irish Supporters club proclaimed: "It is highly unlikely that a foreign man will be appointed. With many people not exactly ecstatic with the present squad containing too many English-born players, imagine the outcry if an Englishman is appointed."

Enter Charlton stage left winning the third ballot ahead of Liam Tuohy. Jack may not have been the unanimous choice, but it seemed be had fewer enemies by the time the intrigue finally subsided. Jack had ruffled a few feathers and made a few points during his managerial career in England with Middlesbrough (twice), Sheffield Wednesday and 15 months in charge of Newcastle United. In some quarters his eventual selection created mayhem. He was shrewd enough to ask the physio Mick Byrne, later a trusted aide, to pick the team for his first match in charge against Wales at home, based on the not entirely illogical thought that Byrne's many years with the team was a good guide to form.

A 1-0 defeat was hardly the best start and Con Houlihan was so disturbed he wrote in the *Evening Press*: "Charlton talks a great game. Yesterday he produced a stinker. This was the pits and in a decent country the spectators would be entitled to a refund. I am tempted to sell my property in Spain and give the proceeds to the FAI. Then they could pay off the manager who never should have been appointed. We have the players. The pity is that Brian Clough has so little interest in fishing." Houlihan, of course, did not know that the team wasn't Charlton's choice and he had many occasions to eat humble pie along with his Guinness. It seemed that Jack did not much admire the skills of David O'Leary the Arsenal centre half, so much in contrast to his own style and ideas of the defensive art. A row ensued and it was three years after the bust-up that O'Leary reappeared on the international scene.

Charlton lured Irish fans away from their other varied sporting interests outside soccer and with a blueprint of moving forward before moving backwards transformed the national side into a formidable force, winning a place in the European Championship finals of 1988 and then blazing a trail into the World Cup Finals of 1990 (Italy) and 1994 (USA) repeating the successes of Northern Ireland under the baton of Billy Bingham who had reached the Finals in 1982 (Spain) and 1986 (Mexico). Lansdowne Road became a stadium of light and enjoyment for reclaimed fans who became enchanted with the "new" Republic team under the command of an Englishman who fished their rivers and won their hearts.

KEANE'S CUTTING EDGE

ROY KEANE'S career with Glasgow Celtic, after 479 games for Manchester United and seven Premiership titles, could not have had a more distressing launch early in 2006 after a 16-week absence from the soccer scene. It was the day a soccer legend's career became a 90 minute nightmare, Celtic being shot out of a third round Scottish Cup tie by Clyde, fourth in the First Division known as the "Bully Wee" to their sprinkling of fans. It was rated the biggest upset since Celtic were bundled out of the cup by Inverness Caledonian Thistle six years previously.

What the bookmakers thought of such a preposterous upset can be gauged from the 50-1 odds at kick-off against Clyde's bringing off the 2-1 coup. Celtic were 2-0 down and all-but out by half time and Clyde had two other goals disallowed. Not a happy day for Keane or Celtic. The defeat challenged Keane, both on the field and off it where he was deft using football "spin" to the advantage of himself and of Manchester United, the team he captained in inspirational style.

Keane's influence extended beyond the pitch into the political arena at Old Trafford following his transfer from Nottingham Forest in 1993. Like Charlton with the Republic, Keane was a man of his people at club level. Keane knew exactly what he was saying when he talked about the "prawn sandwich" brigade. If the cap in the VIP lounge fitted, so be it.

"I don't think some people who come to Old Trafford can spell football, never mind understand it," he said. What he was later alleged to have said in a censored outburst on MUTV about the passion and commitment of some of his team-mates was only part of the story of Keane's sudden departure from Old Trafford "by mutual consent". He was recovering from an injury that might further reduce the pace and power of a 34-year-old who carried deep wounds of his conflict in the heart of the United engine where he was the club's most successful – and outspoken – captain.

Ferguson would never be drawn on who he regarded as his most influential player - Keane, Bryan Robson or Eric Cantona. Although to my mind Keane's closest rival as the most influential player in the Premiership since its formation in 1992-93 is Cantona. Not only did the Frenchman have a widespread vision and ability to create and score special goals; he probably had a more commanding presence able to induce effort in others by his own example whereas Keane drove himself and others to the limits of physical and mental endurance and in doing so, won the adoration of those on the terraces whether they ate prawn sandwiches or not.

Yet it was Keane's fierce will to win that led to his clash with authority and team-mates with his sweeping condemnations that many fans identified as conflict with Sir Alex's trusted and loyal assistant Carlos Queiroz. That public outburst, rather than the leaked venom directed as his fellow players in the autumn of 2005, saw the Old Trafford doors close for the last time. Subsequent disappointing results underlined, even with the Old Trafford faithful, that Keane had a point (although it could be said that the career path of Darren Fletcher in particular was one in the eye for Keane - Ed)

Keane seemed to collect red cards − 11 of them − as often as he picked up medals, seven Premiership titles and four F.A. Cups in his 12 years climaxed by the remarkable campaign of winning Champions League (where he missed the final), Premiership and F.A. Cup in 1999. Even Hollywood, where they know infinitely less about soccer than the pilloried prawn sandwich brigade, could not have dreamed up a more spectacular pinnacle of achievement. Keane drove himself hard (off the field he had to battle against personal demons) and he expected no less of others. Even Ferguson and the quietly-spoken Portuguese Queiroz suffered the sharp edge of Keane's tongue which he should often have bitten rather than unleashed.

Within hours of his departure from Old Trafford, his adoring fans were telling anyone who would listen that their captain had been victimised for telling the truth in his castigations, especially a reference to the "lazy" defender and unnamed player who earns £100,000 and immodestly put himself in the superstar class. It was no surprise when Keane signed for Glasgow Celtic a month's after his bust-up ended 12 years' service. Though Keane was a Celtic man at heart, he originally had eyes on Tottenham Hotspur, dreaming of becoming another Hoddle (hardly his style) or Ricardo Villa (more like it). The first game he viewed on TV was the 1981 F.A. Cup Final with its spectacular demise for Manchester City.

Keane admitted to his loyalty to Celtic in his autobiography. "I was injured and went to Glasgow with a couple of friends to watch Celtic. They were United fans who followed Celtic as well. I had my baseball cap pulled well down over my face. It was great. We had a couple of drinks in a pub near the ground. No one spotted me. As we were walking up to the ground, two big Scots lads took a second look. 'Are you...? You ******* are.' One guy was about six feet tall and built like a barn. 'Hey, big man, when are you going to come and play for a big club?' Big man! He was looking down on me. My pal shot back: 'He *is* playing for a big club.' We laughed. I love the Glasgow humour."

Glasgow clearly loved Keane, with fans spending thousands on Celtic shirts emblazoned with the number 16 within hours of his signature three months after his last game for United at Anfield. Terry Butcher, who arrived in Scotland amid a similar wave of hysteria in 1986, was hardly making an earth-shattering statement when he said he believed Keane would transplant easily. "He's used to the media coverage at Manchester United so I don't see problems for him," said Butcher. But he made a valid point when he added: "There may be the odd referee who wants a Red Card Roy headline for his scrapbook." Punters took up the odds offered by Glasgow bookmakers against such a happening.

Keane's departure further fragmented the treble trophy winners of 1999 to underline the massive input of players needed to create and sustain a club of any standard and emphasised the huge quality in depth required by Alex Ferguson and other managers at the top to try and fulfil the dreams of the Old Trafford faithful. The dream team was shredded thus:

★ PETER SCHMEICHEL: moved to Sporting Lisbon at the end of the treble season and retired in 2003 after stints with Aston Villa and Manchester City and eventually lost his place on the BBC's top TV soccer team.

★ GARY NEVILLE: after seeing brother Phil sold to Everton took over from Keane as captain.

★ DENIS IRWIN: moved on in 2002 aged 36 after sterling service for two seasons with Wolves.

★ RONNY JOHNSON: restricted by injury to only 39 games in three seasons after the Treble winning season, quit in 2005 after spells with Aston Villa and Newcastle.

★ JAAP STAM: abruptly sold to Lazio in 2001 after publishing his autobiography. He joined Milan in 2004 and played in 2005's memorable Champions League final against Liverpool.

★ DAVID BECKHAM: was re-routed to Real Madrid for a "bargain" £25 million (only a quarter paid up front) when his relationship with Fergie soured. Beckham's span in Madrid was not all sweetness and light!

★ NICKY BUTT: quit Old Trafford in 2004 for Newcastle United with his place uncertain. He then moved on loan to Birmingham City managed by his former club-mate Steve Bruce..

★ OLE GUNNAR SOLSKJAER: bravely fought knee injuries for two years and staunchly attempted a comeback late in 2005. (He contributed 11 goals in 2006/7 before joining United's coaching staff – Ed).

★ ANDREW COLE: won the League Cup with Blackburn Rovers, maintaining a goal every three games output there and with Fulham before moving to Manchester City.

★ JESPER BLOMQVIST: was hit by a serious knee injury hampering his career with United and he failed to find his old form with Everton and Charlton.

★ TEDDY SHERINGHAM: switched to Spurs in 2001 and despite being in the veteran class continued to score with Portsmouth and West Ham.

★ DWIGHT YORKE: resumed his duet with Cole at Blackburn in 2002-4 before emigrating to Australia and joining Sydney FC after an ordinary season with Birmingham.

★ DAVID MAY: moved to Burnley for a season in 2003.

★ HENNING BERG: left in 2000 for three seasons at Blackburn before a last fling with Rangers.

★ Ryan Giggs and Paul Scholes stayed put to add to their impressive number of appearances (and eventually their trophy haul – Ed)

★

Keane's outspoken style provoked an untimely outburst on the international stage in Saipan in 2002. Mick

McCarthy, his country's manager, was the target. Keane walked out on the eve of the World Cup finals, critical it seemed of everything and everybody (except himself). That should have been the last chapter of an international career that began in 1991 following his then British record £3.75 million transfer from Nottingham Forest which coincided with United's first League and Cup double.

Yet such was his propaganda technique that within two years, all was forgiven. McCarthy, after enduring what one eyewitness described as "the most articulate, the most surgical slaughtering" he'd ever heard, had gone and Keane was forgiven and back in the Irish team, a hero once more winding up that astonishing international chapter with 66 caps.

One door closes and another opens for men of Keane's calibre. In this case it appeared that the door at Old Trafford was closed, if not slammed, on Keane by a manager who had been happy by developments.

SIX HOURS WITH SIR ALF

IT WAS IN the public domain that Alf Ramsey honestly believed - and he was always honest – that England had the quality of players and the depth of talent as well as the manager to win the Jules Rimet Trophy for the first time since its inception in Uruguay in 1930, despite the British being hailed as the pacemakers and masters of the game. So it came as a surprise when the smartly dressed man who sat opposite me on a train journey from Ipswich to Manchester went one better than exchange pleasantries. Alf Ramsey outlined his blueprint for the forthcoming World Cup of 1966; discussing his hopes in detail, naming players he regarded as being keys in his quest for success and offering opinions on the game in general and England in particular.

The word probably wasn't in vogue then, but I was gobsmacked as I listened to this unaccountably frank 'interview' offered on a plate to a reporter he then knew less than well. He had not discouraged my cautious questions nor scoffed at my humbly phrased submissions about the state of the game and the quality of the players of the day. My queries were timid because it seemed obvious that one word in the wrong place from me would see the curtain descend on an amazingly open stage and the much respected, but hardly voluble, Alf would dry up. Alf, the master plotter, was revealing all to Potter. The England manager loosened up even more as the journey progressed and was virtually gabbling his thoughts, fears and hopes long before Crewe.

My mind was at full stretch, trying to appear nonchalant and unsurprised at his revelations and with no hidden tape recorder as an aide, mentally digest what he was saying and grasp the significance of it. What an interview to stumble across after a night match at Portman Road! "Hold the back page; maybe even with a cross reference from Page One", I thought. If there had been mobile phones then, I would have made an excuse to leave the compartment and warn the office of the journalistic gems to follow. Just shows how important it is to be in the right place at the right time, I mused. YIPEE!

At journey's end, we exchanged farewell pleasantries

and shook hands. I wished "H'alf" (he was prone to misplacing his aitches) the best of luck in his quest and explained that I would not cross his path in the early stages of the tournament as I was assigned to the attractive North West Group (it finished Portugal 6 points, Hungary 4, Brazil 2, Bulgaria 0), working with Clive Toye from our London staff, later to become a top official in the launch of soccer in the USA.

Alf reciprocated my good luck wishes. I was about to bound from the compartment and skip off down Platform One at London Road Station, rather like Morecambe and Wise did in their stage exits when Alf stood erect and suddenly looked taller and wider.

"By the way," he said with a stern face. "H'all I have just told you young man is h'off the record; every single word – strictly." It was a week before I was able to confess to the Sports Editor Eric Cooper, who had the gift of being able to conduct an in-depth telephone conversation while sketching an edition page plan with his free hand, about the journalistic sporting "goal" that never was. My integrity was never put to such a serious test before or after an amazing and unexpected build-up to a World Cup.

Alf was strange if not odd-ball, but his loyalty to his players and skill at moulding teams was without equal. Considering he did not become a pro until he was 24 after achieving his ambition to become a grocer, his record as player and manager was schoolboy fantasy stuff, though his public relations were, at least, unsophisticated. Yet he was scrupulously honest, and later in the Finals he was surprisingly outspoken and direct with his "animals" outburst about Argentina in the quarter finals. That broadside ruffled a few feathers way beyond the walls of Lancaster Gate. The Argentine captain Rattin was sent off after first refusing to leave the field. After the game, Alf banned his players from swopping shirts and quite unlike my placid train companion risked censure and accused the opposition of "behaving like animals."

Alf's boots had done all the talking with the push-and-run Spurs team managed by Arthur Rowe that purred its way to the second and first division title in successive seasons. Southampton, incidentally, had first noted his talent when he was playing with the Duke of Cornwall Light Infantry. Alf's career had major setbacks during the 32 caps he won making his first national appearance in 1948. He was in the team beaten by the USA in 1950 – a defeat that still emerges in soccer quizzes. Sir Alf must have known the end of his international career was imminent when he was also part of the team destroyed by the Hungarians under the baton of the one-footed, multi-talented Ferenc Puskas.

Alf launched into management with Ipswich Town in 1955 and lifted them from the obscurity of the Division Three South to champions of the Second Division in 1961. It seemed to be progression with a minimum of fuss (or so it appeared on the outside, anyway) and then he went on to repeat his triumph by winning the First Division title the next year, three points ahead of Burnley (then playing football with a glow and flow) and four ahead of Spurs, he seemed to have the perfect credentials to become manager of England.

Not so at Lancaster Gate, the HQ of the F.A., where

many heads were inclined to be look the other way when they weren't buried in the sand. But Alf was eventually chosen to succeed Walter Winterbottom in October 1962 and he immediately *told* the F.A. that England would win the World Cup in 1966.

Sir Alf kept his brave promise by making the best use of the players at his disposal, combining workrate with freedom to express talent. It may have cut across the ideology of total football, but the "wingless wonders" rewarded the manager's loyalty to them with performances that gripped the nation. Not all his decisions delighted all of England, especially when he left out Jimmy Greaves in favour of Geoff Hurst in attack; his selection was more of a backing for Hurst than a snub for Greaves. Whatever the logic of the arguments, the West Ham striker's final goal of a 4–2 success in extra time prompted the unforgettable footnote from Kenneth Wolstenholme as a handful of fans swarmed in premature celebration on to the Wembley pitch: "They think it's all over," he said, adding with perfect timing as Hurst's shot hit the back of he net, "It is…NOW."

Wolstenholme was a bomber pilot during the war but like many aircrew had no head for heights outside the cockpit. So acute was his vertigo that he had to be helped, often with eyes covered, on to the gantry high above the pitch before games from where he would deliver his commentary. It was some way off being "all over" for Sir Alf but the Ramsey graph of glory had a few ups and downs before the final dip came in May 1974 when the F.A. slammed the door in his face. Of 113 games at the helm he won 69 and lost only 17.

Despite losing to Brazil in the group stages of the 1970 World Cup in Mexico, England looked to be on course to repeat the success of 1966 with a team widely regarded as more rounded and powerful than that of four years earlier. Ramsey's captain Bobby Moore (Ramsey had worn the captain's armband three times in the absence of the incredibly skilful Billy Wright) was at his peak of perfection.

The door to the semi-finals was nudged open when England were leading West Germany 2-0. Then Ramsey rested Bobby Charlton, presumably saving him for the semi-final, only for the then liberated Franz Beckenbauer to embark on a rampage and England lost 3-2. Such are the variables of sport that Charlton and Beckenbauer became close friends despite Germany beating England again in the 1972 European Championship quarter-finals and then failing to qualify for the 1974 World Cup after a controversial 1-1 home draw to Poland.

Yet it is the Wembley triumph for which Alf will always be remembered. His "wingless wonders" strategy, implanted already in his mind during that breathtaking train trip and explained with excitement on the long journey, was the blueprint for success. Yet we tend to forget how Ramsey tinkered with wingers in the build-up to the memorable final at Wembley. He used width with Roy Stephenson and Jim Leadbeater in his Ipswich championship team. John Connelly (Burnley), Terry Paine (Southampton) and Ian Callaghan (Liverpool) all came and went and many still conjecture that Sir Alf stumbled on his winning formula by chance – more likely it was by a carefully planned trial and error strategy.

Whatever, Alf knew he had key players in Nobby Stiles whose vision was challenged though he never mistakenly clobbered a team mate with one of his lunging tackles.

Jimmy Armfield, whose injury cost him the captaincy on the eve of the finals, used to recall an after-dinner chat at the Hendon Hall Hotel following the success against France and the test against Argentina. Ramsey's companions at dinner were Harold Shepherdson, his team trainer, Bobby Moore and Armfield.

"I casually remarked that I had never seen a really successful England team without an old-fashioned centre-forward, a target man. We talked about past greats Dixie Dean, Tommy Lawton and Nat Lofthouse. I happened to mention that the only big striker we had in the squad was Geoff Hurst. Moore took up the line, pointing out that West Ham always used Geoff as a target man and how he rated him as just about the best in the business."

No-one ever knew if the inclusion of Hurst was in Ramsey's mind but with Jimmy Greaves injured, he used Hurst as a target man against Argentina alongside the dependable and strong-running Roger Hunt. England-Argentina became one of the most notorious matches in the World Cup. For nearly ten minutes the arguments raged on the pitch and the game faced the disgrace of being abandoned before Rattin, the mid-field player and captain, accepted he had been sent off. His eventual departure no doubt boosted the chances of England's eventual win.

Few could argue that despite all the individual brilliance around him, from goalkeeper Gordon Banks to the dynamic Alan Ball, Bobby Charlton was Ramsey's key player. He was pivotal and like Eusebio of Portugal, who was the tournament's top scorer with nine goals, he always seemed capable of scoring match-turning goals. Charlton's brace – his brother centre half Jack was more likely to claim a brace with a Purdey! – against Portugal powered England into the final. Portugal's contribution to the World Cup was immense with Benfica providing stars of dazzling quality in Eusebio, who scored four in a sensational quarter-final against North Korea at Goodison Park. Coluna, Torres, Simoes and Jose Augusto were their other stars.

As Busby and Shankly, among others, had recognised much earlier, Charlton undoubtedly had strong claims to be bracketed with Matthews, Finney, Di Stefano, and Pele as one of the leading forwards in the world.

No excuse is needed for recalling the team that conferred the long overdue 'champions of the world' tag to the nation credited with creating the world's most popular sport. Banks, Cohen, Wilson Stiles (I once interviewed him about his rise to international status in a submarine berthed in Salford docks), Charlton (J.), Moore (capt.), Ball, Hurst, Hunt, Charlton (R.) and Peters.

THE WEST HAM ACADEMY

MANY PLAYERS, MANAGERS and fans would be unable to calculate the debt they owed Ron Greenwood. He was the man behind Sir Alf's success. Without his influence it is unlikely that England would have won the World Cup in 1966.

While many managers advocated a get-stuck-in-philosophy and win-at-all-costs ideology, Greenwood was preaching the gospel of simplicity. "Football is a simple game," he insisted in a statement that can hardly be described as devastatingly revolutionary. "The enemy of the young player is the coach who complicates the game to try to make himself look clever. Football is about the space between two players." Greenwood meant what he said. Without his influence, there would have been no Bobby Moore leading the players up to the Royal Box. No Geoff Hurst scoring the only hat-trick in a World Cup Final. No Martin Peters whose game was some way ahead of the pack. Greenwood's academy at West Ham produced teachers as well as rounded England players. Malcolm Allison, Dave Sexton, Noel Cantwell and John Bond were examples of the coaches who believed in good football.

John Lyall carried on the good work when Greenwood moved "upstairs" before stepping in to fill the gap left by Don Revie's sudden defection to the Arabian desert in 1977. England won 33 of his 55 matches in control, drawing 12 and losing only 10. A notable success came against France inspired by Bryan's Robson's 27-second strike in Spain 1982. Greenwood was proud that England returned from Spain unbeaten when injuries deprived him of Trevor Brooking, another graduate of the West Ham academy, and Kevin Keegan for all but the final minutes of the tournament. Greenwood then drew up a shortlist of those who might succeed him. Don Howe, his senior coach, and Brian Clough, always the people's choice, were among those who aided Greenwood in

Spain.

John Lyall, Greenwood's successor at West Ham, led the tributes when Greenwood died aged 84 in February, 2005. "He believed simplicity is genius...play it quick...play it simple...never leap up to celebrate a goal, because concentration will be lost," reflected Lyall. Sir Trevor Brooking was close enough to know when he said: "Ron was one of the best coaches this country ever produced. I will never forget the things he taught me about the game."

Though the south claimed Ron as their own he was born in Burnley on November 11, 1921 and grew up in poverty in the village of Worsthorne where his father was a signwriter and like many others at the time was often unemployed in the Depression. The Greenwoods wore proper shoes only when going to church. Otherwise they wore clogs with iron bars on the sole. The family fled to Middlesex where young Ron attended Alperton School, leaving at 14 to join his father as a signwriter at, ironically, Wembley Stadium. Ron was spotted playing for a local team and joined Chelsea where he made his debut in December, 1940.

During service with the RAF Greenwood guested, as did many Servicemen, turning out for the team nearest to their base – in his case for Hull City and Belfast Celtic. Chelsea subsequently sold him to Bradford Park Avenue in 1945 and after three years he moved to Second Division Brentford in 1949. Greenwood formed a skilful half-back partnership with a young Jimmy Hill and won a single England 'B' cap before going back to Stamford Bridge. He played for the first half of their championship winning season of 1954-55 – a championship that had to wait another 50 years for a repeat. Greenwood and Hill became disciples of Walter Winterbottom, the first manager of England and his coaching ideology was enhanced by observing the display of Puskas' Hungarians against England in 1953. His reputation as a master tactician soared.

England's qualifying campaign for the 1982 World Cup was entertaining to say the least. The 2-1 defeat by Norway in a vital game in September 1981 produced an often repeated hysterical outrage by a Norwegian commentator who mocked the spirits of Winston Churchill, Lord Nelson and Henry Cooper before proclaiming: "Maggie Thatcher, your boys took one helluva beating."

When it seemed unlikely that England would not qualify for the 1982 World Cup, Greenwood resigned. He informed the team in mid-air as they flew back from Switzerland following another defeat. Yet many players regarded him as a father-figure and a deputation of senior players, led by Kevin Keegan, was sent to change his mind before the plane landed. Only an unusual set of results elsewhere in the group saved England. Elimination in the quarter-finals was a graceful exit, Bobby Robson taking over.

THE BIG SPENDERS

NEW AGE CHELSEA

FOOTBALL TRADITION, and to some extent the format of the Premiership itself, was swept to one side by Chelsea and the multi-millions the Russian benefactor Roman Abramovich was prepared to lavish on the club to see the fulfilment of his outrageous dreams. An endless number of "big" clubs had splashed the cash, not necessarily successfully, to buy success. Such clubs, even the most wealthy at the top of the money tree like Manchester United, Arsenal and Liverpool to name but three, were exposed as mere dabblers in the money game when Abramovich shook his rouble tree in July 2003. It was a new ball game when the unknown Abramovich spent £150 million to buy Chelsea lock, stock and relatively empty barrel; new boy, new toy.

Just to show that he meant big business, within six weeks of taking control at Stamford Bridge, Abramovich spent a further £110 million of his pocket money to buy new players in the biggest spending spree in the history of the game in the UK. Then in his first two-and-a-half years in charge the Russian fished out a further £250 million on new players to become a global big spender willing to put money where his rarely-opened mouth was.

Nothing short of a massive hit wicket by Abramovich or his manager Jose Mourinho seemed likely to stem the flow of success they both craved. The selection of Mourinho to succeed Claudio Ranieri a year after his take-over was another major move in the capital gains game. "The Special One" as Mourinho labelled himself at his first Press conference after taking over, had quickly scaled the ladder of success himself after masterminding the triumph of FC Porto in the Champions League (2004).

It was a shock that England's coach Sven-Goran Eriksson did not accept the chance to jump ship. After all, he had seemed fairly adept at other forms of physical exercise. Or was it so surprising, considering the out-going nature of Abramovich's final choice in a role that might well have left the introverted Eriksson (in football matters, anyway) swept aside by the preparations and motivation required for virtual bi-weekly combat over the marathon course of nine months? The Portuguese gaffer was never reluctant to reveal his thoughts on what was required to ensure continued success at Chelsea, indicating that only his defection or Abramovich throwing his toys out of the pram could threaten the powerful dynasty.

A crumb, relatively, from the financial table of a club of Chelsea's financial structure, would have saved Accrington Stanley from a sad demise in the spring of 1962. None was forthcoming at the time, although Abramovich did sanction a modest gift to help Rotherham United in their struggle against the increasing tide of overheads. Accrington have always been a club with a hint of romance and the football populace mourned its passing with a fixture against Exeter City on 10th March 1962 that went unfulfilled to the dismay of those loyalists who stood on the terraces of Peel Park at a cost of 25p (juniors 5p).

Admission prices soared like players' wages, and so did ambition. But it was not until 2006 that Stanley made a spectacular bid for reinstatement heading the Nationwide Conference with the reward of promotion to League status under the enthusiastic stewardship of the chairman Eric Whalley.

Another Accrington (this time without the famous Stanley name) was part of the Football League's formation back in 1888. Masterminded by William McGregor, a director of Aston Villa, it represented a switch of power from the gentlemen of the south to the working class of the north. From its early days the game's showpiece competition, the F.A. Cup, had been dominated by the public schoolboys of Old Etonians, the Wanderers, Royal Engineers, leaving the northern clubs struggling in their wake. But a switch to rugby by the public schools and pressure from clubs in the north for a definitive set of laws with fixed dates for competition and regular fixtures, eventually inspired the League format with 12 clubs involved without a single entry from the south. The 12 were: Aston Villa, Accrington, Blackburn Rovers, Bolton, Burnley, Derby, Everton, Notts County, Preston, Stoke, WBA and Wolves.

Preston were labelled "The Old Invincibles" for their success in the first season of League combat after being at the heart of the game's first scandal when many southern clubs attributed their success to the payment of "expenses and other inducements" to attract the best players. London's Upton Park complained officially in 1884 and Preston, Burnley and Great Lever were suspended from competition and in a compromise move the F.A. decided to allow professionalism "under strict conditions" and the door to riches galore was opened – John Forrest becoming the first English professional in 1885. Preston romped to success in 1888-89 under the coaching baton of the formidable Major William Suddell. Champions by January, they never lost a game and failed to score just once. Preston did not concede a goal on the way to beating Wolves in the Cup Final to become the first club to record a League/Cup double.

Twas ever thus: "It (the title) has nothing to do with the power of money," Jose Mourinho reflected after winning his first Premiership in Chelsea's centenary year. "It is the power of the players that has got us where we are. They are a group of friends who are prepared to fight for each other." Of course team blending and harmony on and off the pitch is all-important. But, as Major Suddell and the first professionals no doubt realised long ago, it must help to have a bottomless pit of money at your disposal.

A DANGEROUS SPIRAL

Transfer fees and players' pay packets soared hideously out of proportion to talent, the pace quickening rapidly as we entered the 21st century with football seemingly intent on heading for financial farce if not financial suicide. There was hari-kari talk when Chelsea (who else?) were

DAILY EXPRESS Saturday February 4 1984

ANOTHER GREAT EXPRESS EXCLUSIVE

Charlton to join Board in
£10m Old Trafford shake-up

The Red Revolution

MANCHESTER UNITED are this morning locked in a massive £10 million shake-up dilemma.

A package from prestige-seeking millionaire publisher Robert Maxwell that would re-shape Britain's biggest club has already been outlined.

It has yet to be presented formally. But when it is, chairman Martin Edwards will hold the key to the biggest boardroom revolution in years.

Many changes are planned if Edwards accepts £10m for his 51 per cent of the club shares or formulates a deal with his brother director Roger.

He has a 20 per cent stake in the club, taken over by their late father after the Munich air

The changing faces of United . . . Martin Edwards, James Gulliver, Robert Maxwell and Bobby Charlton.

By Derek Potter
The man with the big Soccer stories

since I broke the takeover story in the Daily Express on Thursday : carefully denying he would block a take-over bid.

EXCLUSIVE

Shock bids to buy United

WHAT THE EXPRESS SAID ON THURSDAY

Ryan is the key for new United

JOHN Ryan is set to take on a surprise new role today in a bid to solve Newcastle United's problems — and his own.

The Ireland Under-21 fullback has struggled to justify the £250,000 fee involved in his summer move from Oldham.

And although manager Arthur Cox refused to discuss team plans yesterday a midfield role is being lined up for Ryan. Said Cox : "You'll have to wait and see."

The idea is to re-vamp a side whose lack of physical strength was most cruelly exposed in the FA Cup defeat at Liverpool — and the hope is that it will improve fourth placed United's poor away record.

They go to Fratton Park having lost two of their last seven away matches and it's a match that will give Pompey fans an idea of what it will be like to have Kevin Keegan on permanent view.

John Donoghue

DAILY EXPRESS - 4th February 1984

MANCHESTER UNITED are this morning locked in a massive £10 million shake-up dilemma.

A package from prestige-seeking millionaire publisher Robert Maxwell that would re-shape Britain's biggest club has already been outlined.

It has yet to be presented formally. But when it is, chairman Martin Edwards will hold the key to the biggest boardroom revolution in years.

Many changes are planned if Edwards accepts £10m for his 51 per cent of the club shares or formulates a deal with his brother director Roger.

He has a 20 per cent stake in the club, taken over by their late father after the Munich air crash.

The format for the "new" United would see:

★ *Maxwell hand over control of Oxford United to his family and become the new front man of Old Trafford.*

★ *Edwards retained as £45,000 a year chief executive.*

★ *James Gulliver, a wealthy supermarket boss, already on the board would become vice chairman and backer of Maxwell.*

★ *Former England and United idol Bobby Charlton invited to become a director of the club he helped to make the most famous in the world.*

Several meetings have taken place in secret. No formal draft has been presented by Maxwell's advisers but his anxiety to control a First Division club after savouring the prestige at Third Division Oxford – who knocked United out of the Milk Cup – is the talk of the game.

Informed sources told me last night: "There were one or two interesting switches in United shares before Christmas."

Under Football League regulations 51 per cent off the shares gives control. But it takes a 75 per cent holding or combine to change a club's articles of association.

A deal between the three principles Martin Edwards and Gulliver, make that an easily attainable target.

Chairman Edwards has kept a dignified silence – since I broke the takeover story in the *Daily Express* on Thursday – carefully denying he would block a take-over bid.

But it is virtually impossible for him not to seriously consider a deal that would ensure his family's future and retain his close links with the club.

If Maxwell pushes his deal through it will be the first of many such moves at major clubs where over the years vast earning capacity has been wasted. And there is no more prestigious club in Britain than United.

If Maxwell's bid were successful it could be an embarrassment for United manager Ron Atkinson, who clashed verbally with the Oxford chairman earlier in the season.

Maxwell has great faith in Atkinson's close friend Jim Smith his manager at Oxford and once promised he would want him to move with him.

28/1/1985
DEREK POTTER IS VOTED
BRITAIN'S NO. 1
by MIKE DEMPSEY,
Sports Editor

EXPRESSMAN Derek Potter has been voted British Sports Reporter of the Year by the Sports Council and his fellow professionals.

This most coveted of awards — made by the Council in conjunction with the Sports Writers Association of Great Britain — will be presented at a London ceremony in March.

Bill Hicks, chairman of the judging panel, said : "The judges were greatly impressed by important exclusive stories in Derek Potter's entry and with the added weight of lucid writing he took first place with distinction among the reporters."

Derek's string of exclusives over the year left the newspaper world gasping.

- *HE was the first to reveal that Robert Maxwell was bidding for Manchester United.*
- *FIRST to reveal that Old Trafford chairman Martin Edwards was meeting Maxwell.*
- *FIRST to announce that the whole deal had been called off.*
- *POTTER was the man who announced that Steve Coppell was quitting.*
- *FIRST to tell the Soccer world that Ray Wilkins was going to Italy.*
- *FIRST to tell Britain that Mark Hateley was about to be transferred to AC Milan.*

These are but a sample of 16 nationwide exclusives. Suffice now for us to say that we rejoice in Derek's success, just as Soccer itself does.

He has reached this pinnacle of achievement by hard work, skill, honesty, and by establishing a reputation within the game as The Man Football Can Trust.

SIR LARRY LAMB, editor of the *Daily Express*: "We are all delighted for Derek. His award is richly deserved."

SIR MATT BUSBY : "The award could not have gone to a more worthy man and a great friend."

PETER ROBINSON. Liverpool Chief Executive: "Derek is one of newspapers' great professionals. I am delighted for him."

GORDON TAYLOR, secretary PFA: "Everyone connected with the PFA is delighted. He has always given footballers fair and honest representation."

PETER SWALES, chairman Manchester City: "Well earned and well deserved. And especially nice for me because we come from the same town!"

MARTIN EDWARDS, chairman of .Manchester United: "Derek has always been trustworthy and straightforward. Derek will win more awards with his pen than he will with his tennis racket."

JIM GREENWOOD: secretary Everton "Derek Potter is respected throughout the game and we at Goodison Park are delighted for him."

RON ATKINSON, Manchester United manager: "I rate him as a very knowledgeable football reporter who is more accurate than most."

BOBBY CHARLTON: "I feel privileged to know Derek. He is a credit to his profession and wherever football is the subject he is always on the ball."

EXPRESSMAN Derek Potter, Britain's Sports Reporter of the Year, received his award in London yesterday.

Derek, whose string of exclusive stories left the rest of journalism trailing, accepted his prize from Lord Cudlipp, chairman of the judging committee in an event sponsored by the Sports Council of Great Britain.

Already this year Derek Potter has kept well ahead of the field again. And by the season's end will doubtless turn up with many more Soccer exclusives.

DAILY EXPRESS
22ND March 1985

EXPRESSMAN Derek Potter, Britain's Sports Reporter of the Year, received his award in London yesterday,

Derek, whose string of exclusive stories left the rest of journalism trailing, accepted his prize from Lord Cudlipp, chairman of the judging committee in am event sponsored by the Sports Council of Great Britain.

Already this year Derek Potter has kept well ahead of the field again. And by the season's end will doubtless turn up with many more Soccer

That's more like it!

United revive sagging Soccer

By Derek Potter

IT IS no secret that Bill Shankly once went to the Football Association's coaching think-tank at Lilleshall.

He took over the session from the FA man in charge and then made an excuse and left after an hour. "Shanks" never went back.

Thanks for

DAILY EXPRESS - 28TH SEPTEMBER 1983

IT IS NO secret that Bill Shankly once went to the Football Association's coaching think-tank at Lilleshall.

He took over the session from the FA man in charge and then made an excuse and left after an hour. "Shanks" never went back.

Matt Busby was not all that keen on the coaching manual, either. "Go out and enjoy yourselves," was Matt's mission. United did. And so did Liverpool.

Luckily for our Soccer they did it again in a 1-0 victory for United that suggested the gap between the great rivals is narrowing fast.

It was Soccer off the cuff . . . football from the heart and head . . . but always tinged with discipline and tactical commonsense.

For those fans still hung over from the Wembley nightmare and the coaches clinging to the talent-stifling guff about "long ball" systems and percentages, the clash was a breath of fresh air.

Unlike Bobby Robson, United and Liverpool had players willing to think for themselves as well as fight for others.

Graeme Souness, forced deeper as Kenny Dalglish was pushed back to long range, was inspirational.

So was Bryan Robson. Though short of his peak in the first half, he emerged as the winner of the captains' duel.

United's back four were vigilant and vigorous, though less physical possibly than some Liverpool efforts to stem the flow of football from United in the second span.

Liverpool's supply line was eventually stemmed if not severed leaving Ian Rush (the cobra to Dalglish's shark) short even of the half chances he turns into goals.

If the first half had its turgid moments of feeling out the opposition, the second 45 minutes after the warm-up were blistering.

Finishing in the Rush-Dalglish mould would have seen United home by as many as three or even four goals.

Even so Frank Stapleton's spectacular in the 53rd minute was worth a dozen ordinary goals. Mick Duxbury, Ray Wilkins, and Arthur Graham, a wonderful willing winger on either flank, combined in the best Liverpool (or United) style.

Most United fans wisely delayed their gloating at a third success over Liverpool until the last minute.

It was just as well. The disciplined Marl Lawrenson sent Rush on his last sortie that might well have salvaged a draw for Liverpool.

A Major Blow

One of the saddest stories for a sports reporter to break, is the injury-enforced end to a career. It is all the harder when you know the sportsman concerned, and have first-hand knowledge of how determined that player is.

Steve Coppell had known for some time that his chances of ever again wearing the red shirt of United or the white of England were slim.

A final session in Amsterdam at the special injury clinic run by the Dutchman with the so-English name (Richard Smith) confirmed Steve's fears.

It was a major blow for club and player, leaving a huge gap on the right-wing where he pounded a huge beat with great determination and success.

Pound for pound, Steve was arguably one of the strongest players in the game, and like fellow Scouser Ian Callaghan, formerly of Liverpool, he ran miles in unselfish pursuit of goals and glory.

With him always being the thinking type, it is no surprise that Steve slipped so easily into the manager's chair at Crystal Palace where the chairman Ron Noades said on hearing that Steve had a degree in economics: 'Hell, he's going to want to run the club as well as the team.' Steve is still enjoying the new challenge.

DEREK POTTER
Today

A MAJOR BLOW

One of the saddest stories for a sports reporter to break, is the injury-enforced end to a career. It is all the harder when you know the sportsman concerned, and have first-hand knowledge of how determined that player is.

Steve Coppell had known for some time that his chances of ever again wearing the red shirt of United or the white of England were slim.

A final session in Amsterdam at the special injury clinic run by the Dutchman with the so-called English name (Richard Smith) confirmed Steve's fears.

It was a major blow for club and player, leaving a huge gap on the right wing where he pounded a huge beat with great determination and success.

Pound for pound, Steve was arguably one of the strongest players in the game, and like fellow Scouser Ian Callaghan, formerly of Liverpool, he ran miles in unselfish pursuit of goals and glory.

With him always being the thinking type, it is no surprise that Steve slipped so easily into the manager's chair at Crystal Palace where the chairman Ron Noades said on hearing that Steve had a degree in economics: "Hell, he's going to want to run the club as well as the team." Steve is still enjoying the new

THE STING!

By Derek Potter

DAVE SEXTON and Bob Paisley clashed yesterday on a crunch match issue.

"The next seven days will settle it," said the Manchester United boss.

"Saturday will decide nothing." replied the Liverpool leader.

Sexton made his claim after watching United close the gap at the top of the First Division

BOOM

DAILY EXPRESS - 31ST MARCH 1980

DAVE SEXTON and Bob Paisley clashed yesterday on a crunch match issue.

"The next seven days will settle it," said the Manchester United boss.

"Saturday will decide nothing." replied the Liverpool leader.

Sexton made his claim after watching United close the gap at the top of the First Division to four points by winning at Palace while Liverpool crashed at Spurs.

"That sort of talk is silly because after Saturday there are six games to go," said Paisley.

Liverpool visit Old Trafford on Saturday after Stoke go to Anfield and United travel to Forest in midweek trials of character and strength.

Ridiculous

And Paisley, striving to whip Liverpool to a 12th title win, four ahead of next-best Arsenal, added: "The only certainty is that we won't win anything if we don't play better than we have done in our last two games.

"Performances like these make talk of being certainties to win anything ridiculous. Tottenham was our only defeat in six games in March, but no-one can make excuses. It was an undisciplined performance lacking our normal character."

But it is easy, though, to understand Sexton's seven-day theory. United must not fail at Forest on Wednesday and must beat Liverpool.

Sexton made his ambition plain when he said: "We're still thinking in terms of winning every match. It was a tremendous boost to win at Palace and it keeps our momentum going..

★

After a 0-2 loss at Forest, United beat rivals Liverpool (2-1), the start of a 6 game winning streak that took them to the top. Sadly a 0-2 defeat to Leeds meant that they lost out to Liverpool who claimed their title 12th league title.

★ ALL the tension of the Manchester Derby typified by Malcolm Allison, pictured by Expressman Milton Haworth, as he leapt out of the Old Trafford dug-out to make a point to his City on Saturday.

THE LAST THROW!

DAILY EXPRESS - 24ˢᵀ MARCH 1980

MALCOLM ALLISON yesterday launched a last desperate offensive aimed at keeping Manchester City in the First Division.

His aim is a Maine Road offensive against fellow relegation strugglers, beginning with Bolton next Saturday.

"This game may be more important than Saturday's derby," said Allison yesterday.

"We have got to win our home games to stop other teams getting close to us."

City also meet Everton and Bristol City at home in a crucially important month, but they have already beaten three of the relegation pack – two of them, Bolton and Everton, away.

Allison, who predicted a City win at Old Trafford, brushed aside the "you are going to get the sack" taunts from the Stretford end.

"They were only chanting because they are frightened to death. I will do them again, eventually," he said.

"I was more disappointed with our team work against United rather than individual performances. We should have got that together by now."

Meanwhile United match-winner Mike Thomas last night revealed his derby secret . . . that stomach trouble had practically wiped out his week's training.

"I'd given up the ghost about playing. I just didn't expect to get into the side," he said.

"When the boss told me I was in I was shocked. I thought I'd blowed my chance by doing no proper training."

Thomas had a total preparation of one reserve game. "It was my first with United and I didn't like it one bit. There was no atmosphere," he said.

★

Manchester City drew, 2-2 with Bolton Wanderers, 1-1 against Everton and defeated Bristol City 3-1 in those vital home matches.

City finished the season three places and six points above Bristol City who were relegated along with Derby County and Bolton Wanderers. John Bond replaced Malcolm Allison as Manchester City manager later that year.

strongly rumoured to have re-kindled their interest in Andriy Shevchenko, AC Milan's Ukranian striker and European Footballer of the Year. A world record fee of £30million for one footballer? Was the game going into orbit? Could it be only 100 years, you wondered, since the first £1,000 transfer took Alf Common from Sunderland to Middlesbrough. It was 1928 before the transfer spiral soared to a fee of £10,000 when David Jack, whose nephew was a successful journalist, was transferred from Bolton Wanderers to Arsenal.

Old pros must have gasped when Chelsea dangled an offer of £30 million-plus for Steve Gerrard, who eventually re-signed for Liverpool launching himself into the ranks of top earners while Rio Ferdinand stalled over a new contract at Manchester United with a salary topping £100,000 a week (or £5.2 million pounds a year).

Soccer, it seems, hurtled down the route that could lead to riches or ruin in the U.S. where the top players at American football, baseball and basketball earned at least two to three times the pay-off of our soccer stars. It was reported that Peyton Manning, a quarterback with Indianapolis Colts, netted £20.1 million for his skills while Shaquille O'Neal, the giant Miami Heat centre, mopped up £15.9 million. Alex Rodriguez, New York Yankees third baseman, had to be content with a mere £15 million.

Gerrard played cat and mouse with fans and club, handling his case before and after the absorbing Champions League Final success with dodgy diplomacy. Jamie Carragher, another product of the Anfield academy, signed his contract extension without a murmur of dissent after displaying a consistency on the field that made him captain material.

It was difficult to rationalise the financial trend. But it seemed to most observers that wages and transfer fees outstripped talent. Loyalty is another question. Ferdinand had a particularly strange attitude to it by apparently overlooking the fact that United paid his salary in full without him kicking a ball in anger for eight months while he was suspended for failing to take a drugs test. Ferdinand, some said, was the most stylish central defender in England. They obviously never saw Bobby Moore and many, many more like him. Nor did they see the likes of Harry Johnston, Stan Cullis, Neil Franklin or Joe Shaw. The list of players who would be today's big earners is endless. They could be forgiven for reasoning that the game surrendered to the urges of greed, dishonesty and thuggery even.

PLAYERS WIN PAY BATTLE

IT IS DIFFICULT to assess the cloak and dagger role eventually played by players' agents in the crazy pay spiral from the day in 1961 that the players bound free of the financial restraint on their talent, originating from the formation of the Football League in 1888. Figures released by the Football League revealed that by 2004, the clubs spent £7.8 million on agents' fees with Leeds United shelling out almost £1.9 million. Many clubs at the grass roots of the game would doubtless find such figures mind boggling, being left to guess at the drain from the secret society of the Premiership where the spin-off from contracts worth in the region of £5m pounds a year can only be estimated.

Back in 1961 the crucial meeting that led to the liberation of the players from restrictive shackles was in Belle Vue, Manchester under the chairmanship (or should that be "chinmanship?") of Jimmy Hill, the elected chief of the Professional Footballers' Association.

Jimmy later sampled life on the other side of the fence as a manager with Coventry City and as chairman of his old club Fulham before launching a successful career in TV. One impassioned speech questioned the "immorality" of footballers being paid more than miners.

"My dad's a miner earning £10 a week," one player said, "I play in the lower divisions and I can earn twice as much. I train in the open air and play football on a Saturday. Dad's down the pit for eight hours at a time, five days a week. That can't be right. We earn quite enough as it is." Strangely, a number of members of the Professional Footballers' Association shared that soft-line thinking, in stark contrast to the gun-at-the-head strategy that was later to hold the game to ransom.

The case 'for' was staunchly put by Tommy Banks of Bolton Wanderers and England's left back in the 1958 World Cup. "I'll answer that," said Tommy, part of the Hartle, Banks, Hennin, Higgins and Edwards defence that could, at the very least, be described as formidable. "Now then, son, tell thi father from me, I can do his job. In fact, I've done it. And so can any one of these lads in this hall. But if thi father wants to know why we want more brass, tell him to come and play against Brother

Matthews in front of 40,000 fans. That's why we want more money."

"Brother Matthews" backing had helped to win the fight. Jimmy Armfield, who won 43 caps between 1959 and 1966 and captained England 15 times, was above average as a player. But his club Blackpool were below average in finances and support despite being part of the formidable Red Rose brigade that once graced the First Division – Preston, Burnley, Blackburn Rovers, Everton, Liverpool, Manchester City and Manchester United made up the Lancashire hot-pot. Armfield's pay doubled to £40 a week and the footballers' lot became a happy one. Or did it?

When it was reported that Johnny Haynes was to be paid £100 a week at Fulham, the first to be so lavishly rewarded, the press went into overdrive. Armfield, later to be a colleague on the *Daily Express*, demanded, and got, a rise of £5 a week. It was the same Armfield who dared to tackle his boss Joe Smith about his earnings of £16 a week in winter and £14 a week in summer when Matthews earned £16 all the year round. "Matthews is a better player than you," Armfield was told. Jimmy agreed, adding, "but not in the summer, he isn't." Some so-called big money earners (not necessarily deservers) may well be better players in the summer!

For all that the boot is now firmly on the other foot, footballers were undoubtedly enslaved until 1961. It is no exaggeration to say that players can now hold the game to ransom as the proportion of English players in the English Leagues dwindles. Only a few months after his £17 million pound transfer from Real Madrid to Newcastle United, another outfit some way off its peak, the proceeds of Michael Owen's record deal were revealed. The England vice-captain emerged as the highest-paid player in the Premiership with a basic £102,000 a week and gross earnings of £5.3m per year, outstripping the previous highest financial haul of Frank Lampard, claimed *Four Four Two* magazine. Lampard, who signed a five-year deal with Chelsea worth a mere £90,000 a week, was rated joint 13th, with team-mate John Terry in the Rich List Top 20 Players headed by David Beckham (£75million), Dennis Bergkamp (£37million) with Owen (£30million) third in the list. How times had changed!

Yet despite these outrageous salaries it still came as something of a shock to learn that England star Wayne Rooney had agreed a five-book deal charting his life in football earning him a minimum of £5 million only four months past his 20th birthday and with less than three full seasons as a Premiership player behind him. The record-breaking contract more than doubled the amount paid to a British sports personality and swamped the £2.1 million paid to Rooney's international captain David Beckham. Other, more established, England players like Michael Owen, John Terry, Rio Ferdinand, and Frank Lampard trousered about £1 million for their life stories, a similar fee to that paid to Sir Alex Ferguson and the controversial Roy Keane for their memoirs.

A search began to find a ghost writer or writers at a much reduced rate of pay capable of developing a relationship with Rooney and extracting from him the kind of in-depth information required for his literary marathon. Rooney, whose career was in the stars from an early age, had a limited education with just one GCSE pass. His development from a "yer-know, boy–done-well" level of interviewee would be put to a gruelling test – for his ghost.

THE BOSMAN BONANZA

HUNDREDS A WEEK became thousands a week, thanks to the revolutionary Bosman ruling that gave footballers equal rights of employment enjoyed by the general workforce. It meant that players were free to wander where they pleased at the end of a contract, though the European Commission watered that freedom down by ruling that players could only move in two transfer windows a year. As predicted by the judge responsible for the Bosman transfer edict, the restructuring of the system clearly benefited the fat cats and pampered pussies who play the game, but how they compare in quality with their predecessors is another story.

Ten years after the landmark victory, Jean Marc Bosman, the Belgian player who took on single-handedly and beat the bosses of the dictatorial UEFA, found himself jobless and shunned by the game he liberated in 1995. "People never understood what I was doing. Others did everything they could to stop people understanding. I was the anonymous guy who dared to attack the system. I would have preferred that someone else fought the battle." Bosman had an unspectacular career in the Belgian league and ten years after the end of his five-year fight through the courts, he felt shunned by the football establishment. "The only environment

I want to work in is football. But I feel that I'm not welcome there. It seems I was always a nuisance."

Not only did the players cash in on their new freedom, their agents flourished in the slipstream. Business boomed for the agents, many of whom failed to remove themselves from the shady corners of the game. Jon Smith was always regarded as an admirable agent before and after his personal salary explosion. He was a founder of the First Artists agency which conducted some of the biggest deals in Europe, placing players with clubs who had no transfer fee to pay and were thus able to line the pockets of the players and grease the palms of those who did the spadework for them. "The Bosman ruling handed players sizeably more power and it was the cornerstone of the football agents' business," he admitted, "imagine the chaos if traffic lights no longer existed from tomorrow. That is what happened to football. Players run their contracts down and this causes panic." Some deals were gems for club and player. Others fell as flat as a dive in the penalty area. Here are sample success-failure stories.

★ Gianluca Vialli stepped into Chelsea boots and won the Cup Winners' Cup, F.A. Cup and League cup as player and manager.

★ Teddy Sheringham, once of Manchester United, travelled on successive free transfers to Spurs, Portsmouth and West Ham and was still scoring golden goals while nudging 40.

★ Sol Campbell staggered Spurs fans by moving to arch-rivals Arsenal when his contract ended. Campbell's form at Highbury merely added to the anguish.

★ Edgar Davids, goggles included, boosted Martin Jol's re-building task at Spurs.

★ Jay-Jay Okocha took French leave from Paris Saint Germain and delighted "Trotters" fans at Bolton with his uninhibited trickery.

★ Winston Bogarde joined Chelsea from Barcelona only to start just two League games in four unhappy years in West London, softened by his payslip of £40,000 a week.

★ Patrick Kluivert failed to take goals to Newcastle, scoring only six in 25 League games, all for £60,000 a week.

★ Markus Babel was kept out of the Liverpool defence by illness for a year and before falling out with manager Gerard Houllier.

★ Michael Reiziger appeared rarely in Middlesbrough's defence after injuring his shoulder immediately following his arrival from Barcelona.

★ Mark Bosnich, having been given his chance in goal by Manchester United, fouled up another big reprieve with Chelsea.

HAYNES FIRST TO A HUNDRED

IT SEEMS POINTLESS to compare one generation of players with another. Even so, it is impossible to resist trying to guess at the money the artistic Johnny Haynes would be worth a week as the players pay packets exploded to new peaks from the year 2000. Tommy Trinder, the Fulham chairman, kept his promise to make Haynes the first ton up boy of soccer once the minimum wage system was scrapped. Haynes was poetry in football motion; a conductor raising the standards of the musicians under his control with hardly a demonstrative gesture. It used to be worth the admission fee, fans said, just to watch Haynes warm up for a game he could control without any recourse to emotional outbursts, dirty tricks or theatrical gestures.

It always seemed unfair that he did not join the knights of football or receive a mention in the Honours system for the expertise that wrecked defensive systems, notably in Fulham's record 10-1 win against Ipswich Town in 1963. Italian strategists were already working hard on defensive strategies before Haynes touched his peak of perfection. They saw Haynes as the key to open big doors. Tottenham, in their financial heyday, would have answered any ransom fee demanded by Fulham to take Haynes across London. Photographic evidence remains of a transfer move challenging recent proportions, when Newcastle United were prepared to pay the earth − £60,000 was the earth in the 1950s − for a Fulham trio consisting of, inside-left Johnny Haynes, inside-right Bobby Robson and centre-forward Bedford Jezzard. They were photographed on the steps of Craven Cottage, the beloved football home of "Gentleman Johnny" Haynes, where the quality of his long range passing plundered so many crucial points for Fulham and goals and space for the likes of Jezzard, the whimsical, unpredictable Tosh Chamberlain and Maurice Cook.

Robson rejoined Fulham in 1962 after a spell with West Brom to find himself being paid half the wages lavished on Haynes. "That doesn't mean you're twice as good as me, you know," Robson often recalled telling

Haynes, adding, "Johnny was always the jewel in the crown." Such a precious gem had to be hidden when he arrived at Fulham as a 16-year-old in 1950. He was a year too young to be officially recognised as a professional player, so Fulham gave him a job as office boy. Of course, he spent more time training than penpushing for a year with the knowledge of the club of course, and many more which used similar strategies until boys could turn professional at 17.

Haynes happily played his 18 winters in England before "grazing" on the pitches in South Africa where he won his only medal, before retiring to Edinburgh with his Scottish wife. Though Haynes won nothing in the English game, his achievements in keeping Fulham afloat for so many seasons in the top rich seam of League football were adorned with recognition on the international scene where he appeared 56 times for England scoring 18 goals between 1954 and 1962. The highlight was surely leading England to the 1961 Home Championship with a famous 9-3 rout of Scotland, the magnitude and significance of which did not prevent him eventually settling down north of the Border!

Haynes played his last game for England, previously handicapped by the loss of key players Roger Byrne, Duncan Edwards and Tommy Taylor who perished in Manchester United's Munich air crash, in the 1962 World Cup campaign in Chile. The door to glory that England had so far failed to fling open was finally slammed shut by the legendary Brazilians. Despite injury in a car crash, Haynes was able to weave his magic with Fulham for a further eight years, but the leg problems reduced by a crucial fraction the level of his pace and impact on the international stage.

Even so, his influence as a player and as a captain helped England to finally win the World Cup in 1966. Haynes had steered Bobby Moore through the 1962 campaign and by his example as captain had laid down a blueprint for his successor who finally held the Jules Rimet cup aloft at Wembley in 1966. Like Haynes, Moore had the valuable asset of composure to use alongside enormous natural talent evidenced by the bonus of 'time to play' seemingly bestowed on all truly great players in all sports. How players like Haynes and Moore so often found themselves in open spaces to give or receive the ball is best ignored by the less able.

★

WHOEVER RAN THE advertising campaign for Brylcreem had his head screwed on by enlisting the services of two sporting icons – Haynes and the charismatic cricketer Denis Compton. Haynes was the David Beckham of his day, except that it can be staunchly argued that his ability, his temperament and his coiffure outstripped the inconsistent and eccentric styles of the boy from Leytonstone. Like so many high profile footballers, Haynes was a good and keen cricketer, rejecting a contract with Middlesex to join Fulham. He enjoyed the company of cricket's Sir Garfield Sobers as much as his later knighted football team-mates Bobby Charlton, Bobby Robson his manager Alf Ramsey and his captain Bobby Moore.

Few players subsequently missed the financial

open goals presented to them, thanks to Haynes and his Fulham team-mate Jimmy Hill in the scramble for lavish contracts with thousands available to spend on cars of the most powerful and prestigious varieties in the showroom with speeds way above the maximum allowed on British motorways.

Not only should the pampered, lavishly-paid Premiership players be grateful to their brothers for their earlier crusade. They might, perhaps, spare a thought for those who played north of the border. Those inclined to enjoy a joke at the expense of those Scots who, to say the least, have, and indeed often enjoy, a reputation for frugal dealings, should spare a moment to consider the plight of Stewart Imlach whose son Gary provided a moving account of his father's experience at the tight-fisted hands of the Scottish F.A.. Imlagh Snr. won an F.A. Cup winners' medal with Nottingham Forest in 1959 and played on the left wing for 423 League and Cup games without a blemish on his disciplinary record for all of £20 a week. Stewart played once for Scotland in 1958 during the World Cup in Sweden where the squad were denied even £2 a day out-of-pocket expenses and any kroner advanced was later deducted from the meagre match fee. In a money-saving strategy, caps were awarded only to those players who represented their country in home internationals.

"Football was a game of the working class, for the working class, by the working class," Gary Imlach wrote in his award-winning book My Father And Other Working-Class Football Heroes. Stewart Imlach was devastated by the failure to recognise his appearance and would have happily paid for a cap. He died without it despite his son's continuing campaign in the hope that the more advanced-thinking SFA might award a cap posthumously in memory of his father.

When Jimmy Hill announced the deal and the ending of the unjust pay capping, he said: "I have made it quite clear to the players that they have to put all their energies and enthusiasm into improving the game. We have told the League that we will back them 100 per cent in disciplining anyone who behaves badly."

The discrepancy between that pledge and the situation decades later is something the modern game should question. It is appropriate to recollect the occasion before the financial boom when I spotted Chris Lawler, a highly accomplished and unflappable right back for Liverpool and England, standing in a bus queue a mile or two from Anfield. He gratefully accepted the lift uncomfortably close to the time when he should have been reporting for match duty, as unruffled then in his predicament as he always was on the pitch.

Haynes would tell you how much he fancied playing on perfect surfaces with the lightweight ball introduced after his retirement. He would have had fun; entertainment was guaranteed. Haynes once recalled. "I remember one season when Fulham scored 100 goals and didn't come top. We couldn't work it out until someone pointed out we had conceded 100 goals as well. It was great fun, wasn't it?" Not only was that statement an appropriate epitaph for a great player, it was a reminder about the real purpose of playing and watching football.

EXCLUSIVES

MATTHEWS THE MAESTRO

SOMETHING IN THE tone of his voice alerted my news sense. "Mandy Hill is preferred to *me* for the game on Saturday," opined Sir Stanley Matthews with a detectable emphasis on the "me". This, I reasoned, is transfer talk - even at the age of 46! I ran the story the next day and within 48 hours, Sir Stan had left Blackpool and rejoined Stoke City. It was the opening paragraph in the final chapter of a remarkable career of a player who often trained along on the sands near his Blackpool home, with ozone and carrot juice as the basis of his remarkable longevity. Needless to say, he never smoked or drank alcohol. Dozens of games later, aged 50, insisting that he had quit too soon, Sir Stan finally hung up his special lightweight boots (made by CWS Manchester - normal boots then were clog-like with steel toecaps) to aid the surge in pace over the crucial 15 yards that would send him past any opponent of any age.

The return of Stan to his native Potteries was a triumph for Tony Waddington, an average player with above average vision who transformed the shape and future of Stoke City with his audacious moves into the transfer market, often for players who had been "scrapheaped" or who were attracted by Waddington's unorthodox blueprint.

Waddington, a Mancunian and on the junior staff of United pre-war, tried to model himself on Sir Matt Busby, with a drastically more slender budget and staff. In Gordon Banks, Stoke had a goalkeeper whose save from the Brazilian master Pele in the 1970 World Cup is still regarded as one of the greatest-ever. He made adventurous signings for Stoke, probably best pleased by the silky skills of Jimmy McIlroy, a pivotal player in Burnley's heyday when their scouting system produced a seemingly endless supply of talented players, the craft of Dennis Viollet, the pace of Peter Dobing and the guile of Alan Hudson among many quality players nearing the veteran stage.

Waddington also recruited with a touch of the unorthodox at the young end of the game. He invited Garth Crooks to have a full blown trial after watching him play football in the street outside the Victoria Ground near Garth's home. Crooks also drew attention to himself by breaking a window and repeatedly kicking the ball against the wooden doors at the Victoria Ground. Crooks later moved from Stoke to Spurs in 1980 for £80,000, taking part in the F.A. Cup Final a year later and also in 1982. Crooks later joined the TV circus when his playing career ended following spells with Charlton, Manchester United and West Brom. Presumably Crooks inherited his media instincts from Waddington, a master of public relations who signed a journalist, a former colleague Derek Hodgson, as his assistant. But it was the signing of Matthews, the first footballer to be knighted, that was the talk of the game in 1961.

Stan had left Stoke in 1947 for £11,500, a fairly small

fee even then, to join Blackpool where the F.A. Cup Final of 1953 was the highlight of Matthews's career when little Ernie Taylor supplied the passes and Stan Mortensen plundered a hat-trick with Bill Perry scoring the goal that finally deluged Bolton Wanderers 4-3.

Sir Stanley was shrewd. On one occasion the Blackpool squad arrived in London for a game without Stan, who was given carte blanche to arrange his own travel and fitness regime, an arrangement that continued under Tony Waddington, unlike the rigid programme imposed on Sir Tom Finney by Cliff Britton at Preston. The former plumber later revealed that not being able to modify his training reduced his career span. Hours before the team was due to leave its hotel, Sir Stanley had not yet arrived at the London headquarters. Mandy Hill was told by the manager that he was playing as stand-in for Stan. A few hours before kick-off a pink-faced Stan swirled into the lounge where manager Joe Smith immediately enquired about his fitness. "No problems, I'm fine, boss" responded Matthews. Smith turned to the bemused stand-in and told him: "You're not playing, son – Stan's back."

What Matthews had not revealed was that he had just then returned from a jaunt to an African outpost, where he made a guest appearance for some wealthy prince and had returned to the team hotel in the nick of time faintly tanned and wearing an assortment of expensive looking jewellery. And though he was by no means fully fit after the unofficial game and exhausting travel, he camouflaged the injury with yet another crowd-pleasing, top class performance.

Like many high class performers in sport and the arts, Matthews was tense and nervous before games. Any match remotely above the ordinary, he once revealed to me, was invariably preceded by a visit to the loo to be physically sick. Many footballers of Matthews' generation famously learned their trade with a tennis ball in the streets around their homes. Stanley went one better. He would persuade the local butcher to give him a pig's bladder and pursue the inflated sphere, playing his own version of the wall game. His accuracy at crossing the ball, dangerously heavy when wet and less inclined to swerve than the modern 'beach ball', was incredible and it was always said that he never kicked the ball behind the goalline from a corner in 34 years as a league professional. The old cow hide ball weighed the same as the modern plastic one (14 to 16 ozs) at the start of a game but by the end it could double in weight having absorbed water from the pitch.

Matthews had played his first international against Wales in Cardiff as a 19-year-old in 1934 and his last against Denmark in a World Cup qualifying game three months after his 42nd birthday. Stan played almost 800 league and cup games for Stoke and Blackpool. He never accepted the commonly understood accolade that the 1953 final was "The Matthews Final." It was, he always insisted, with an emphatic statement of the obvious, a team game. Where would Blackpool have been in that remarkable summer of 1953 without the three goals Stan Mortensen rifled past Bolton Wanderers? Or the skill of Ernie Taylor, who was a mere 5ft 5in tall, weighed around nine stone, smoked and enjoyed a drink, in stark contrast to the football knight he partnered so succesfully on the right wing?

Blackpool also had a stick of rock in their defence by the name of Harry Johnston, the captain. Anyway, the success for Blackpool (and Matthews) was in the stars, so to speak. After all it was the year when Everest was conquered, a young Queen Elizabeth was crowned and Sir Gordon Richards won his first Derby. It was also the year, it is worth recalling, when England won back the Ashes and Trevor Bailey became a national institution, not for his capacity to score runs at a pedestrian pace, but for his ability to remain at the crease. No wonder they called him "Barnacle".

Many believe that Matthews was the greatest footballer of all time and 150,000 lined the streets of Stoke to pay their respects on the day of his funeral, 3rd March, 2000. It was hardly surprising that thanks to Stan, Blackpool were the most attractive visitors in Division One for seven successive years. 'Gates closed' signs were habitually hung outside grounds an hour before kick-off as a tribute to the pulling power of one man. Though he was, of course, blessed with more than his fair share of natural talent, Matthews worked harder than most to achieve and retain his fitness. He had strong legs, a thin body and the balance of ballet dancer. The secret of his success he declared was "Work and practice. Practice. Practice. Practice." Many veterans of football have subsequently made the charge: "Players don't practice enough these days."

Of course, Matthews was a perfectionist. He was also a hungry fighter as they say, deprived of lush training facilities, his mind was similarly uncluttered by coaching dogmas where the 'tracksuits' talked confusingly about such obscure technicalities as POMO – position of maximum opportunity. It is doubtful if Matthews would understand such a mind-boggling theory never mind be concerned about how to put it into practice in a game of instinct. His background was the Potteries where his father was a barber and an amateur boxer from whom he no doubt inherited his speed, agility and the mental toughness to always be in control of his emotions. When a full back tried to kick Matthews out of a game, he knew he had won the first round. The knock-out quickly followed. It was matador versus bull from then on. Once Matthews whizzed past a defender there was no second chance.

DENIS THE MENACE

FATE BROUGHT TWO of the giants of my generation into contact (and almost conflict) at Huddersfield Town where Bill Shankly was a journeyman manager and Denis Law an unknown teenager. Denis was overdue to report back for training after the summer break. As Shankly impatiently awaited his return, he rehearsed with his coach Bill Young the admonishment he was to deliver for Law's unexplained late return to Leeds Road. Eventually the scrawny son of an Aberdeen fisherman arrived and knocked timidly on the manager's door. "Come in," snarled Shankly. Then, completely forgetting his rehearsed words of chastisement for his boy wonder, he grasped the be-spectacled skinny Scot by the hand and said, "Great to see you son – welcome back", for Shanks knew he held a football diamond in the palm of the same hands that had once sorted coal as a cherrypicker at Glenbuck in his native Scotland.

Eventually Denis was sold to Manchester City for a record £55,000 in 1960 and the following year he went to Turin for double the fee to become the first British six figure player. In 1962 he was back in Manchester, joining United for a British record fee of £115,000, going on to score a record haul of goals for Scotland and in the heat of Cup and League combat at club level. Law, lethal and belligerent on he pitch, was kind, shy and ever-helpful off it. On one occasion I had invited Tommy Docherty to be guest of honour at my old boys football club. Before the dinner, a telegram announced that Tom was regrettably unavailable."

I had the inspiration and the nerve to shoot off to Denis's home just round the corner from the venue in Bowdon and ask him if he would be a last minute substitute. The Laws were getting the children ready for bed. "I'll be there in ten minutes," Law said without a reference to the ill-timed, outrageous request. He changed from evening casuals into sharp suit and arrived as promised to a standing ovation for his generous gesture by a bunch of amateur players who would have paid pounds just for the honour of cleaning his boots. There was never a hint of payment for the gesture. How times were to change when players became sensationally over-commercialised. Docherty kept his promise the next year to join a list of stars and ex-stars who gave their time to give pleasure to others. The Doc's singing of the Sheikh of Arabee in a duet with a totally relaxed member of the Old Alts club was one of the highlights of one merry evening.

What was not known in 1962 was that Denis turned down the chance of trousering £20,000 – a mighty sum then, and not that bad at any time, come to think of it – to join Juventus instead of United.

No player, surely, has been more blatantly approached illegally than Law. By none other than Sir Matt Busby himself! Law was picked to play for the Italian League against the Football League at Old Trafford. Sir Matt, accidentally I am sure, bumped into Denis at the banquet after the match. It was man to man.

"How do you like playing in Italy, Denis?" asked Sir Matt, knowing the answer, of course.

"I don't like it," replied the ever-candid Denis. "Why don't you come and buy me?" A crazy chase across Spain and Switzerland followed before Matt finally got his man – the 17-year-old he introduced to the Scottish international scene during a brief reign as national manager. Such a blatant "tap" would have evoked big headlines in later years!

Even so, it was common for players to be "tapped" from the early days of the game, as Sir Matt himself discovered. Chelsea are by no means the only club to have "accidental meetings" and make arrangements through a third person. It can be safely assumed that everybody in the game, F.A. and League officials, club directors, managers and players knew how much the "tap" or illegal approach was always part of the game.

IN SEARCH OF BEST

GEORGE BEST WAS a difficult player to find on the field as his team-mates and opponents quickly discovered, and even more difficult to track down in his private life as Manchester United and the media pack soon discovered after his sensational arrival on the Old Trafford scene. So it came as a major shock to be told by the office: "George has gone missing again – he's somewhere in Majorca." George had gone AWOL in the latest of a series of brushes with authority. One 'crime' was to write a newspaper article without permission and failing to turn up to join United for a game in Israel after going AWOL for a Northern Ireland international about a year after Busby handed over to Frank O'Farrell.

To find a needle in that particular holiday haystack was a task to be faced with considerable trepidation. A travel company executive at Manchester Airport who, also coincidentally, was friendly with a former Manchester United player, had instantly offered her co-operation and supplied a ticket on a holiday flight that night to Palma for which, to the best of my knowledge, the *Daily Express* never received an invoice. The seasoned traveller, with many miles under his seatbelt, caressed an iced Scotch and sat back on the half empty Comet smugly observing the nervous quirks of some fellow passengers, many, I suspected, on their maiden flights and considered the hazards of my dodgy assignment. Most importantly of all, I wondered if George would co-operate – if I managed to find him. At the start of the descent south-east of Madrid, the Comet hit violent, unannounced turbulence. Veteran traveller Potter rapidly shared the anxiety of his virgin flyers and was brought down to earth literally and metaphorically rather less smoothly than he expected, to begin the search.

Sherlock Holmes, surely, could not have faced a more challenging piece of detection work, especially considering the lack of background information to boost the search. But thanks to the help of a travel company official at Palma Airport (a kindly Ms Byrne whose father coincidentally was a gateman at Old Trafford) I was, to my amazement and relief, soon on course to locate Mr. Best shortly after my dawn arrival in Majorca.

A few hours later a handful of pesetas loosened the tongue of an aged, sleepy, friendly figure squatting on the steps of an apartment block in the morning sunshine of Magaluf. He tilted back his battered sombrero and, sure, he knew where "El Beatle" was in hiding. A blue bikini inched open the apartment door. "Who wants him?" she asked closing the door before returning to announce, "he'll meet you in the Barracuda Bar on the beach at ten-thirty."

Any of the numerous news journalists who were obliged to trail Best around his Manchester nightspots hours after the sports reporters had done their work, could be excused for calling it a day and retiring to the nearest bar with a case of San Miguel, forlornly accepting that they were in for a very long wait. But I had to give it a go, so with my mind in a scrambled mess I moved to the Barracuda bar trying to assess the odds against Bestie showing up or understandably embarking on another runner with the stunning blonde in the blue bikini. Yet to my astonishment and relief, George *did* show up eventually, only half an hour or so late, looking remarkably fresh and more alert than I expected in the circumstances.

Was my slick sleuthing, aided by two chunks of outrageous luck, about to have a pay-off? I ordered drinks of course – a small one for him and a large one for me - and began to quiz George tentatively at first about his latest defection from Old Trafford. We talked on and off the record and I delivered a personal message from Sir Matt Busby gleaned by my Sports Editor Mike Dempsey. George gave frank and sometimes diplomatic answers to my questions and I thanked him for honouring his promise and fled to the airport pondering on the journey: Was blue bikini to be the new permanent girl in Best's complex love life? That's another story, I mused as I urgently phoned my exclusive to the *Express* and within 36 hours of my hurried departure, I was back in Manchester.

Shortly after my link-up with George, he too was back home and happy to be re-united with United. It had been a lucky mission from an unpromising start. Later I was to learn that United's management had decided that it would be the end of the road for Best had he failed to return from his latest defection.

It had not taken a genius to recognise the talent in the skinny kid from the sprawling Cregagh estate in east Belfast whose father Dickie was convinced his son was "too small, too lightly built" to make a footballer. Albert Topping persuaded Best senior to let George play for Cregagh Boys' Club. There he was guided by Hugh

"Bud" McFarland who encouraged Best's expression on the pitch and ruled that such natural talent did not require formal coaching. Amazingly, Best was not invited to be a member of the Northern Ireland schoolboy team by selectors who considered he lacked the necessary physical attributes. McFarland found that ridiculous and challenged the schoolboys to a friendly match which they won 2-1 with Best outstanding.

Bob Bishop, who represented Manchester United in Ireland, ran his own team called Boyland. They lost 4-2 to Cregagh Boys Club with Best scoring twice. Bishop dispatched Best to Old Trafford on a two-week trial with another hopeful Eric McMordie. They arrived on the Tuesday, were immediately homesick and Best was back in Belfast with McMordie by the Thursday. Best returned at his father's wishes and signed for United with chief scout Joe Armstrong in August, 1961 and became a part-time clerk at the Manchester Ship Canal Company until he could be signed as a professional at 17. The rest, as they say, is history. Best played 37 times for Northern Ireland and McMordie made it, too.

By the late sixties Best was a global star with solid claims to be Britain's outstanding player. But how could his genius be measured even by those lucky enough to have watched play "live" or observed on film such giants as Stan Matthews, Tom Finney, Alfredo Di Stefano, Ferenc Puskas, Pele, Johnan Cruyff, and Diego Maradona? Best's balance, speed and ability to score goals with either foot or head was a lethal cocktail of talent, probably summed up best of all when someone said: "If Best had been born in Brazil, we would never have heard of Pele."

It is tempting to ponder how much better a player Best might have been in different personal circumstances, especially if he had the self discipline shown by so many of his global rivals. May be we never saw the best of Best. Or with tactical restraints he might have become no more than an average player. What it is not difficult to recognise is the extraordinary skills Best inherited and developed from being a toddler with a ball at his feet, head cocked to the left even then as it was in all his 466 games (178 goals) for United. His debut on 14th September, 1963 against West Brom came after only three reserve team matches. Such a brief apprenticeship for the youth with the spindly physique, indicated the confidence Sir Matt had in the signing from Belfast four months earlier. Pitches were often mudheaps in 1963, partly due to the ravages of a severe winter that shut the game down for months. There was no hiding place against defenders who clattered before they chatted early in Best's days. Arsenal had Peter Storey, at Chelsea there was "Chopper" Harris. Tommy Smith ran the arena at Anfield and at Leeds United if Norman Hunter didn't make the cruching tackle, it might well be Billy Bremner or Jack Charlton who was always around to pick up the pieces, metaphorically that is.

Defenders were allowed to tackle from behind very often at thigh height in a manner that would frighten all but the bravest. A strong, feisty left back called Graham Williams, spent much of the first half trying to impress on Best that he had chosen the wrong job at the wrong time and in the wrong place. Best even nutmegged Williams without showing a trace of humility before Sir

Matt switched him to the left flank and out of the firing line.

Williams said it all when he later asked Best to stand still so that he could study his face. "I want to know what you look like because all I've ever seen of you is your arse disappearing down the touchline," he said. That view was to become a familiar sight for multitudes of taunted defenders until Best played his final game for United against Queens Park Rangers on New Year's Day, 1974, aged 27 years and four months. That he was someway off reaching his peak as a player and could have expected to play for another five years presuming he escaped the attention of the hatchet men, underlines the quality of his talent and the extent of its dissipation.

There is a strong case with hindsight for wondering how his career lasted so long, rather than find its short duration a surprise. After all Best had been through the card of ways in which to reduce athletic prowess. The celebrated boxing trainer Angelo Dundee once said of Muhammad Ali that "every day is like a new toy to him". That was how Best approached every football match and it could also be said it was how he viewed his philandering. It was seemingly the lack of a new peak to scale after his role in the success of winning the European Cup in 1968 that blunted the soccer scalpel. Best scored a typically audacious solo goal that night of magic at Wembley against Benfica and he was named European Footballer of the Year for his exploits in a victory made possible by Alex Stepney's save that deprived the talented Eusebio at a critical stage of the final.

The Portuguese had been dazzled by the Best magic

sleight of foot two years earlier in one of his best games in a European Cup quarter final. Best scored twice in a 5-1 win and his heroics earned him the title of "El Beatle." United travelled to the Stadium of Light, where Benfica had never lost a European game, with a 3-2 lead. The atmosphere was electric with the fans setting off a barrage of flares and firecrackers, their passions enhanced when the mighty Eusebio was presented with the European Footballer of the Year trophy. Best scored an early goal with a header before adding a sensational second "gliding like a dark ghost past three men," in the words of Geoffrey Green in *The Times*, before guiding the ball past the goalkeeper. With a theatrical flourish, he landed back at Manchester Airport wearing a magnificent sombrero. Busby reflected: "I told them to play it tight. George just went out and destroyed them. He was a law unto himself." Best was all of that to his sad end in a London hospital and a farewell by an estimated 15,000 at his funeral in Belfast.

It was not until some time later that Sir Bobby Charlton and Denis Law could be regarded as close pals of Best, despite their mutual dependency. "I had been brought up to play a certain way for the team and I wasn't always sure how to regard a team-mate who could do so much on his own," Charlton once recalled. "We hadn't seen a footballer like him before and no-one who lived like him. I remember how he'd give that charming grin when I told him about annoying me in a game against Nottingham Forest. He hadn't passed the ball to me all match, so I decided that when he next got it, I wouldn't run to make myself available for a pass. George got the ball and when I stayed back he was forced to weave one way, then the other and back again. I sat back thinking I had made my point, muttering 'that'll show you you greedy so and so.' George just went on and stuck the ball in the net!

"Looking back years later, I always thought Manchester United learned from having George around. The club recognised that sometimes you have to make allowances for special players. We treated Eric Cantona differently and, maybe, if we had leaned a bit George's way, it might have changed the way things turned out. Who knows?"

That professional distancing which grew into a growing and lasting friendship, was initially due to both Bobby and Denis, who worked hard to build and maintain their game at the highest level for club and country, having more than a passing distaste for the manner in which Best mistreated his own genius, failing to acknowledge that his rare talent was worthy of respectful preservation.

"If they didn't give me the ball I always knew Paddy (Crerand) would," Best said in a flash of humorous pique. Once, when questioned about why he had failed to pass to either Law or Charlton at a critical stage of an attack, he quipped back "because they were off-side!" Best also said in another broadside: "I started thinking about United and myself after we won the European Cup. I think we were one of the worst teams to win it. I got pissed off because I thought United should have built a team around me and not Bobby Charlton." United's poignant return to the scene of their success in

Lisbon in 2005, somewhat eerily soon after Best's death was the subject of prolonged speculation and the size of failure was calculated in tens of millions. Even Sir Alex confessed to being "in deep shock" as he undertook some urgent stocktaking.

Six goals in a cup tie was the club record Best set in February, 1970, in an 8-2 destruction of Northampton Town. Best's last goal was not only a statistical record for his club but remarkable in its delayed execution. After rounding goalkeeper Kim Book, Best stood on the ball on the goal-line and saluted his adoring fans before prodding it over the line. Sir Matt, whose column I ghost-wrote for the *Daily Express* in the early sixties, would confide, strictly not for publication, about the problems of controlling the personal life, rather than the task of harnessing the talent on the pitch, of a devastatingly handsome and intelligent young man who rarely refused an autograph and who responded to telephone calls and visits to the digs he shared with another United prodigy David Sadler at Mrs. Fullaway's home in Chorlton-cum-Hardy, by invariably first inquiring about the caller's welfare.

In his way, Best psychoanalised his boss rather than being the subject on the couch. "They sent me to the psychiatrist after I'd run away for the first time, or was it the second I can't remember. He asked dafter questions than some of the journalists I know and that's saying something. When Matt sent for me to give me a bollocking I used to count the animals behind him on his office wallpaper. One day he was really mad at me and I managed to count them all – 272 animals."

Despite his activities off the pitch, Best trained as hard as any of his talented team-mates. Goalkeeper Harry Gregg, fellow Northern Ireland international recalled: "He never missed training and he never shirked a tackle and if people tried to kick lumps off him, he'd kick them back. He was as brave as a bull and as nimble as a matador bouncing the ball off the nearest foot, knee or backside and darting off with it." In training he kept possession of the ball so often that two-touch football gave way to one-touch. So George often played the first touch against a team-mate's legs and like a pinball footballer cannoned his way through defence towards goal.

Reporters not involved directly with football were on nightly stand-by to chase stories about Best's latest escapade in his nightclub Slack Alice or at his bachelor pad he built in the suburb of Bramhall which was more like a goldfish bowl than a personal retreat. Those scribes spent hours of frustration chasing Best around the hotspots of Manchester, so when he quit so prematurely they had a party to celebrate his departure and the end of their zany missions. To their professional dismay, Best turned up again not long afterwards playing for Stockport County a few miles outside Manchester! It was a only a three-match stay at Edgeley Park before Best moved on again and began to race down the path to his demise on 25th November, 2005, aged 59 in hospital surrounded by friends and family with the world cursing his demons and praising his genius.

Sadly, Best failed to fulfil his ambition of playing on he greatest stage of all – the World Cup finals. Nevertheless George Best was *the* best. He even wrote his own epitaph when he said: "I spent loads of money on birds, booze and fast cars. The rest I just squandered." A United fan put the later breed of superstars in perspective when he claimed with a grin: "Wayne Rooney? Not fit to lace George Best's drinks."

PLAYERS

GREAVES THE ACE GUNNER

WHEN IT CAME to goal sniping, none could challenge the skills of Jimmy Greaves. "Jinking Jimmy" rarely challenged the bludgeoning skills of Bobby Charlton or Roger Hunt who were always capable of ending a lung-busting run with a spectacular drive yet Greavsie was a defender's nightmare… a razor sharp poacher with a marksman's eye similar in style to Ian St. John of Liverpool who he later partnered in a successful TV duo as "The Saint and Greavsie." The show went on for several years with St. John underlining his verbal versatility. I knew at first hand about the Saint's co-ordination skills. St. John was casually flipping a coin in the air and catching it as he sat at a bar musing about the day just ending. I flicked out my hand and intercepted the coin before it reached his palm. He smiled, clearly impressed by my snatch, and challenged: "Beat this, then." He flipped the coin way above his head, 'caught' it on his outstretched right foot, launched the coin into the air again and dropped it into the outstretched top pocket of his blazer. The challenge was not accepted!

It took a lot of 'bottle' for Greaves to rampage through the record books. It is ironic, then, that Greaves's biggest triumph was to give up the bottle. That came through a former colleague Norman Giller (a Fleet Street drinker) of the *Daily Express*, a huge fan of Greaves and a personal friend for many years. The friendship reached a mutually rewarding peak on Jimmy's 38th birthday on 20th February, 1978. The pair celebrated by deciding to give up drinking. Both have been teetotallers since.

Greaves scored an amazing 357 First Division goals and his 57 games for England yielded 44, an incredible average. Three times Greaves burgled five goals in a match and scored on his debut for every team he played for at club and international level. He topped the First Division goals charts for six swashbuckling seasons. It hardly seems remarkable that he should score on his international debut against Peru in Lima in May, 1959. It took a brave manager to sideline such a rapier goalscorer. Yet after playing in the first three games on the way to England's success in the 1966 World Cup, Greaves gashed his shin against France and was replaced by Hurst. Sir Alf Ramsey – brought up in Dagenham like Greaves – kept an unchanged team, Hurst scored a memorable hat-trick in the triumph at Wembley. Greaves missed the after-match cup-waving on the balcony not in a fit of pique, but to fulfil a previously arranged family holiday in Majorca before rejoining Spurs a week later on their pre-season tour of Spain.

Such impressive Greaves goal stats should either make modern players blush, drive them to drink or merely be regarded as a statistical tribute to a phenomenal player at his most lethal, probably, when scoring 124 goals in four seasons for Chelsea before moving to AC Milan before returning to England with Spurs. He became homesick, but hardly as sick as Serie A defenders who saw him score nine goals in ten matches, before winding up his career with West Ham for two seasons. Greaves' chief attribute was instinct, anticipating slips by defenders before they were made. Ian Rush had the same nose for goals during his highly productive spells with Liverpool, netting 346 times.

Stats, of course, do not reveal the true calibre of strikers. But it was interesting to note after the 2004-5 season an up-dated goals-games chart showed that Michael Owen's 32 goals for England came at a ratio of 0.45 per game, ranking him seventh in a list headed by Vivian Woodward in 1903-11 whose 29 were scored in a 1.36 ratio when goalkeepers were either visually challenged or enjoyed a drink. Greaves clocked in at 0.77, Nat Lofthouse 0.90, and Gary Lineker 0.60.

GOAL-THIEVING MAGPIES

MAGPIES, WE ARE told, have a challenging, almost arrogant attitude that wins them few friends. They are also highly intelligent, very adaptable and are popular with farmers because they eat harmful insects and rodents. In spring, large numbers of magpies often gather to sort out territorial conflicts and social standing. A bit like St. James Park, except that the gathering takes place from August to May each year. And it is not every year that the Magpies have much to crow about. Season 2005-06 was nothing less than traumatic for, arguably, the most loyal and vocal supporters in the game. Michael Owen's injury was a major setback for Graeme Souness as well as the player, lured from Real Madrid under the noses of an apparently indifferent Liverpool during a £50 million spending splurge by Souness in the ever-inflated market. Sven Goran Eriksson later revelaton, in his "fake sheikh" interview, that Owen went to St. James' Park "for the money" hardly came as a surprise.

Freddy Shepherd, the United chairman, also fell for a "fake sheikh" sting some time before Sven. This time the exposé was all about happenings off the pitch which were of a nature not unfamiliar to Sven himself. The combination of Owen and Alan Shearer was an alluring spearhead they hoped potent enough to steer the Magpies from surging turbulence and preserve the status of the manager. A 3-0 defeat at Manchester City was the last nail for Souness, who had fallen a long way short of being able to translate his cultured gifts as a player to those under his command. Shearer's breaking of Jackie Milburn's record of 200 League and F.A. Cup goals was an upside to a sordid season. It was not all that bright for the other clubs in the North East bracket. Sunderland had a catastrophic season; Middlesbrough stumbled. The two provided one moment of magic – on the terraces. "Going down, going down," chorused the Middlesbrough fans as Sunderland were heading for yet another defeat. "So are you, so are you," responded the Sunderland supporters with an immediate riposte.

Milburn was a name on everyone's lips; a blur in black and white stripes when he set out on a goal hunt. You didn't have to be a Magpie fan to have on instant recall the names of Geordie giants like Frank Brennan, Bobby Mitchell, Corbett and Cowell and little Ernie Taylor. They were giants of the F.A. Cup with a magnificent winning treble. Magpie fans called Milburn "jet" as a tribute to his scorching pace. Despite being tall, 'Wor Jackie' was not as strong in the air as Shearer. Milburn was probably more versatile, able to use his pace on the right wing to devastating effect, terrorising full backs in brash runs to the by-line. Milburn and Shearer were different in style and physique, sharing the accuracy and skill to put the ball in the back of the net. Shearer was what they call a "footballing centre forward" enabling other players to feed off his ability to hold the ball and use his compact and strong body to take him wide or, if necessary, backwards. Often it was speed alone that took Milburn into the target zone. With Shearer it was often sheer strength.

Milburn flouted tradition. Despite his proficiency and fitness he was superstitious and he was a heavy smoker. His pre-match routine once involved eating a meat pie and he carried an elephant charm in his shorts. He wore the same tie during the club's three successful F.A. Cup campaigns in the 1950s. Milburn supplemented his income by taking part in professional sprinting events and also worked in the local pit until he was 25. After retirement Wor Jackie became a football reporter and when he died in 1988 aged 64, the city came to a standstill for his funeral.

Many compared Milburn to Thierry Henry of Arsenal who topped Cliff Baston's long-standing League record with his 151st Premiership goal the same night defeat ended the sad Souness regime. He was the fifth manager in 12 years to take the helm at Newcastle United, a statistic that questions the wisdom of those who made, and paid for, decisions that failed to give the fans what they wanted and richly deserved – success on a major scale. Shearer's decision to delay his retirement for another 12 months helped to ease the anger of the fans who had questioned the decision to fire Sir Bobby Robson and replace him with Souness whose team finished 14th in the Premiership after Sir Bobby had steered Newcastle to fourth, third and fifth, with a place in Europe for three consecutive years.

So once again the directors raided the piggy bank for a reported £3 million, to compensate yet another manager – who they appointed in their wisdom – for his failure. Such financial suicide merely underlined the cash awash in the game, with so much of it flowing in the wrong direction into the open sea. What other profession rewarded failure with such lavish pay-offs? How could directors in any other industry survive? But football is a tough world, not a career for the faint-hearted or for those with a nervous disposition. Managers and coaches are judged on the bounce of a ball. They are branded geniuses or idiots on the result of the last game while directors are able to sack good or bad bosses and damage reputations just to save their own skins. For every hundred players who would never fail to give one hundred percent, there will always be a number of shirkers and a sprinkling who will find unexpected ways of letting themselves or the club down. The game is a goldfish bowl, even in big cities like Liverpool, Manchester, Birmingham or Newcastle unlike London where miscreants can mingle unnoticed should they choose.

It is revealing to compare the Premiership records

of the five selections by Freddy Shepherd, the chairman, and Douglas Hall, his notional deputy:

Kevin Keegan (1992-1997): P143 W78 D30 L35
Kenny Dalglish (1997-1998): P56 W19 D18 L19
Ruud Gullit (1998-1999): P47 W11 D18 L18
Sir Bobby Robson (1999-2004) P188 W83 D51 L54
Graeme Souness (2004-2006): P56 W16 D17 L23

Geordie fans have had their share of successful strikers, but can there ever be another like Milburn or Shearer whose style and output seemed destined for consumption only at St James' Park? Malcolm Macdonald had the pace and strength of Milburn and Shearer that generated incredible roars of pleasure and enthusiastic support from fans who knew a striker when they saw one. Mick Quinn and Les Ferdinand also had their moments of magic on Tyneside. Those fortunate enough to have observed two giants in live action are unlikely to see two more such lethal marksmen at one club even in half a century.

Twenty eight days after equalling Milburn's all-time club record, Shearer finally claimed goal number 201. It underlined Newcastle's first League success in more than a month, but perhaps the more interesting statistic was that the Toon Army in attendance numbered 51,627 to watch a club in chaos with a player on the threshold of a scoring record.

Many Newcastle fans will have cast expert eyes at Anfield where strikers seemingly arrived in an endless procession. Luck as well as finely honed judgment has a part in successful dealings in the transfer market. Liverpool needed every bit of help when finding a striker player to replace Kevin Keegan. Not only did they succeed, they found a carbon copy in Kenny Dalglish. Both had pace, tight control, balance and a hawk eye for goal. Neither was tall – Keegan the shorter at only 5ft 7in – but pound for pound as they say, they punched, in the football sense that is, as hard as anyone before or since. I recall, Bob Paisley confiding after he lavished a club record £440,000 on Dalglish in the summer of 1977, "We have found another Keegan." Many believed that Dalglish, with an average of a goal every game with Celtic, had even more variety to his game than Keegan, replaced so soon and expertly after his departure to SV Hamburg and further glory on the continent.

It had seemed that Liverpool would never replace the duo of Ian St. John and Roger Hunt. They did in Keegan's more forceful and more successful partnership with John Toshack; a Little and Large pairing. At 6ft 2in, Toshack towered over Keegan by seven inches – a tricky combination for opposing defenders – and they read each other's game with a remarkable intuition and instinct, Keegan scoring a century of goals in their partnership, the big Welshman notching the remaining 95. Scunthorpe United, as it had done earlier for goalkeeper Ray Clemence (another Anfield recruit who rose to international status) was the home of Keegan until Bill Shankly made his transfer bid in May, 1971.

Shanks had stalked Keegan for some time before his offer of £35,000 was accepted. Another revealing financial aspect of the transfer was Keegan's pay packet. At Scunthorpe he was earning £30 a week, plus £8 for a win, £4 for a draw. He persuaded Liverpool to pay him

£50! What a pay-off in Keegan's first game; 51,000 saw him score a goal, win a penalty and shine throughout a 3-1 win over Nottingham Forest at the start of season 1971-72. Dalglish, naturally, scored on his debut against Middlesbrough in an instant bonus for Paisley who had previously raided Scotland to sign two more giants in Liverpool's history, Alan Hansen and Graeme Souness.

Dalglish devoured the record books, playing a record 102 times for Scotland with 30 goals to equal the output of Denis Law, remarkable for a nation not renowned for its scoring prowess in subsequent years. Dalglish was 26 when he arrived at Anfield and had the durability to make 515 appearances and score 172 goals in a Liverpool shirt. It is hard to dodge stats when looking at Paisley's record with Liverpool who he joined before the last war, resumed when hostilities ceased and as player and manager racked up eight championships, three European Cup successes, two F.A. Cup triumphs – Liverpool had never won the trophy until 1965 – and four League Cup successes for good measure. And he was never really that keen on becoming manager!

The size of the transfer fees paid for Keegan and Dalglish represented exceptional value in quality and length of service. Strikers traditionally hunt in pairs. The pairing of Dalglish and Rush was breathtakingly lethal and like Keegan and Toshack there was a considerable contrast in height. Rush, aged 18, arrived from Chester amid surely the most arduous cup semi-final of all time. Liverpool and Arsenal slogged it out through four meetings and two periods of extra time in a tie that spanned almost three weeks. Rush arrived almost unnoticed during the marathon struggle which Arsenal eventually won only to lose the final to West Ham, Trevor Booking scoring the only goal. Rushie rattled up a club record of 346 goals from 660 senior appearances (a ratio of .52 goals per game) in two spells at Anfield, split by a year in Italy with Juventus in 1987-88. His haul of medals was sensational: five championships, one European Cup, three F.A. Cups and five League Cups.

Rush's 44 goals in the F.A. Cup had statisticians drooling over the biggest haul since the 19th century! He also hit a record five goals in F.A. Cup Finals and he shares a 49-goal record in the League Cup with Geoff Hurst. And to prove he scored goals for fun, his 47 first team goals in 1983-84 is the highest by a Liverpool player. His record is schoolboy comic stuff though aerial combat, unlike the towering Toshack, was not his forte: he netted five in a game against Luton, scored four in a match three times and amassed 16 hat-tricks. Defeat by Arsenal in the 1987 League Cup final ended another amazing personal stat: Liverpool had not lost a total of an incredible 144 games when Rushie scored. Rush also hit a record 28 goals for Wales and played his last game when he led Liverpool out at Wembley for the 1996 F.A. Cup final against Manchester United.

John Aldridge was another prolific marksman to grace the Anfield stage, scoring a total of 329 League goals for Newport, Oxford United, Liverpool and Tranmere Rovers. In all competitions for those clubs he scored 410 goals in 737 games and a spell in Spain with Real Sociedad yielded 45 goals in just 63 games. There was a spell when it seemed Robbie Fowler - known as

'God' to Koppites – could not miss the net. He notched 171 goals in 330 games (a strike rate of half a goal a game) before he moved on to Leeds United in a £11 million transfer in 2001 and subsequently to Manchester City signed by Kevin Keegan, where the goal graph and performance level dipped disappointingly. His career path was similar to Michael Owen, another darling of the Kop, who was surprisingly allowed to drift to Real Madrid where his career hit the buffers and then on to Newcastle United.

Liverpool always seemed to know how to find and deploy strikers, preferably hunting in pairs, stressing the need to have strong goals potential so vital success and in hiding any defensive deficiencies. After allowing Owen to move to Newcastle instead of tempting him back to Anfield, six months later Liverpool did invite Fowler to return to the home he had left unhappily in 2001 when Gerard Houllier packed him off to Leeds United. Fowler's punch in the 1990s saw him plunder 120 goals in 236 League games and secure a place in the Liverpool hall of game.

MERCHANTS OF MENACE

SPEED IN FOOTBALLERS comes in all sorts of shapes and sizes: rapid acceleration over the first few yards, sustained pace at speed, acceleration in later stages of a run and in the lucky and rare players a combination of all three. Those whose surging pace I always found exciting included Stan Mortensen of Blackpool, Jackie Milburn (Newcastle United), Gerry Francis (QPR and Manchester City), Ivor Broadis (Manchester City,

Newcastle United), Roy Vernon (Everton), and latterly Paul Gascoigne, Eric Cantona, Craig Bellamy, and Thierry Henry to name some random examples. Some of the surges by Wayne Rooney certainly equal any by Paul Gascoigne who he so closely resembles in style and build. The pace of Best and Charlton would delight the managers and fans of any generation. Despite his frail-looking figure, Vernon was capable of long, lacerating runs and was a key figure when Everton did a "Chelsea" with Harry Catterick buying success with the John Moores investment, modest by today's standards but considerable at the time.

Everton battled through the snow and ice to scoop the First Division title in 1963 (previous success 1939) as a prelude to an amazing span of successes on Merseyside and abroad with Liverpool rampaging through the honours books. Few can claim to have ever witnessed a more formidable and fascinating mid-field trio than Alan Ball, Howard Kendall and Colin Harvey, who made his debut as an 18-year-old against Inter Milan in the forbidding San Siro stadium to successfully and nervelessly take on the power and stealth of Suarez, the ace in the Inter pack.

Everton always seemed to be anxious travellers abroad. That was never more clearly exhibited than on one sortie into Europe when the players, the night before the return flight home, frog-marched BEA Captain Johnny Walker from the after-match party, to his bedroom. Their anxiety about drink intake by their pilot was totally unfounded, although that could not be said of all players, media and officials. Vernon was not the only Everton prankster. Goalkeeper Gordon West pulled off one injury-feigning coup that makes today's tumblers and fallers novices in the art of deception. Like many players, especially goalkeepers, West had lost some front teeth. After one goalmouth scrimmage, he pointed to the gap claiming he had been punched in a melee. Much time was wasted of course as West and the referee searched the mud and grass for the 'missing' tooth, which was safely attached to a partial denture back in the dressing room. "You don't have to be mad to be a goalkeeper, but if you are – it helps," was the message that went with the trade.

Similar examples of "gamesmanship" and theatrical reactions to tackles and challenges continued to haunt the game with no apparent strong arm disciplines from the authorities despite numerous promises.

Harry Catterick had been poached from Sheffield Wednesday to manage Everton where he shrewdly took instructions from a friend in politics about the art of avoiding direct questions from the press and answering in a general or side-track style. Like Busby before him, Catterick was spinning long before politicians knew the meaning of the word. Catterick was a modest striker himself with Rochdale but with the cash flow available he bought and blended well. Catterick wanted "hard men" in his team, complementing the dainty skills of Alex Young, another player with blowtorch acceleration, he added the rugged qualities of Denis Stevens, Jimmy Gabriel and Tony Kay.

Even 'hard man' Catterick, who claimed that John Harris, later to manage Sheffield United, concentrated on applying his elbow to a painful carbuncle on Catterick's neck in one match as a diversion, made excuses for Young. Severe problems with foot blisters restricted Young's training routine

★

PLAYERS CONTINUE TO fling themselves to the ground as if riddled by a hail of bullets to win a free kick from the conned referee. It always seemed to be essential to roll over several times as if one stage from a death twitch in an attempt by the drama queens to make a mountain out of a molehill. Such activities were worthy of a scholarship to RADA, or at least a place in pantomime as our game descended inevitably to the laughable antics that plagued the game in Latin countries many years earlier. There seemed to be a calling to have special judges equipped with cards, as in ice skating or ballroom dancing, to award points for the originality and quality of the performance. Diving hit the headlines again with a performance worthy of a maximum six for a spectacular dive, as if felled by a heavyweight punch, when Arjen Robben went down after a slap from burly goalkeeper Jose Reina during Chelsea's demolition of Liverpool. One renowned commentator mischieviously advocated that the cheat of the season should be honoured. He even suggested an approach to the swimwear makers Speedo to sponsor a Diver Of The Year award.

Rafa Benitez put his finger on the Stamford Bridge clown incident, so to speak, when he captured the mood perfectly in a post-match interview. "I'm in a hurry because I must go to the hospital because the injury (to Robben) was so serious that may be he will there for a week," he said. "You can see on the TV he will be three weeks in the hospital with the neck broken." An earlier attempt by the F.A. to clampdown on diving apparently fizzled out, no doubt influenced by the difficulty of proof. A club lawyer might easily claim that the player he represents is, in fact, a big girl's blouse with an appallingly low pain threshold and therefore there should not be a case to answer. In defence of the authorities it should be pointed out that any number of players in the Premiership could be banned at any given time if sanctions were applied, thus robbing the public who pay their wages of the privilege of seeing them in regular combat. The tradition of pistols at dawn rapidly became replaced by handbags at 3 o'clock.

Diving and time-wasting became irritating issues which escaped a rigid response from the authorities. So imperative became the need to win that teams enjoying a slender lead or hanging on for a precious point became expert at "running down the clock." Apart from feigning injury, prolonging substitutions (whether necessary or not), spending an age over goal-kicks and throw-ins (and allowing the ball to slip through fingers requiring it to be repossessed), placing free-kicks in the wrong place so they must be re-located, some teams always seemed to be seeking other ways of reducing the actual playing time.

One unofficial estimate put the time wasted at 40 minutes but the scandal went unchecked by the F.A. in deciding against the lesson in other sports where there is a fourth official whose tasks include time-keeping. That would relieve referees of guessing how many minutes should be added to compensate the fans for time "lost" from the 90 minutes they paid astronomical prices to watch. A case for the Trades Descriptions people?

So many managers, especially in the Premiership, have a touch of paranoia. We constantly hear about conspiracy theories in after-match "we wuz robbed" interviews where their team would have won except that a handball claim was ignored or not seen, a blatant off-side was not observed, a penalty not given, or a red card awarded instead of a free-kick. Had the managers watched the same match? The referee clearly had not.

Goalies, whose often costly mistakes are there for all to see (blunders in other positions especially in mid-field pass unnoticed) rarely escaped criticism in the media, on the terraces and in the dressing rooms. It has never been recorded which comedian first labelled a goalkeeper "Douglas" after the wartime air ace, Douglas Bader who flew with courageous efficiency wearing artificial legs made of tin following an accident. "Brilliant in the air – iffy on the ground," was the cruel message. A number of goalkeepers have been branded "Cinderella" for "always missing the ball." Tommy Lawrence, whose sorties from his goal-line introduced a new dimension in the Liverpool defensive strategy of the early sixties, was less cruelly than it sounds labelled "The Flying Pig" by Everton fans because of his considerable bulk, though they always had a soft spot for the Scot who won three caps between 1963-9. Lawrence was something of an athletic freak in that he joined the unusual group who put weight on during pre-season training and lost it through the summer when he was less disciplined in his eating and drinking habits.

Managers had their moments of descriptive colour, notably when Peter Crouch joined Liverpool and was described as having the control "of a giraffe on roller skates." Years earlier the same description was applied to the much-travelled Derek Dougan whose eccentricity included shaving his head long before the bald look became trendy. Before Dougan left Blackburn Rovers, where he caused as much administrative mayhem as he did to opposing defences, the manager who used the "giraffe" put-down made an unsuccessful attempt to sign him before Aston Villa succeeded! Dougan went on to win 43 regulation size caps for Northern Ireland.

It took Crouch an age to score his first goal for Liverpool, but he eventually doubled his PL output while thousands of miles away in Japan; surely a cert question for a sports quiz. It was decreed by the mysterious Dubious Goals Panel that a Liverpool goal in their 3-0 win against Wigan at Anfield ten days earlier should be credited to the developing Crouch though the ball only crossed the line thanks to two separate deflections by Wigan defenders. The DGP made the decision presumably with the aid of modern technology though such usage in contentious riot-inducing issues like "did-the-ball-cross-the-line?" was frowned upon by officialdom. It seemed that the DGP acted on the age old premise that if the ball wasn't going into the net before it was deflected, it should be an own goal. In Tokyo, the gangling Crouch's frame (all 6ft. 6in of him) not only dwarfed the locals, but proved to be more of a hilarious talking point than it had in his native Cheshire and at his previous clubs Aston Villa and Southampton.

HORSES FOR COURSES

RACEHORSES AND GREYHOUNDS have riffled the wallets of many famous and not-so-famous footballers over the years. Racing was not only the sport of kings, it was the sport of men whose lineage was less regal. Pete Leigh, former captain of Crewe Alexandra and not adverse to a modest punt himself, took Stan Bowles under his wing at Gresty Road towards the end of a football career laced with a liking for the turf – racehorse turf. "I got him down to tanner Yankees," was Leigh's proud claim.

Mick Channon had a special gift for a second career that never became apparent even to the shrewdest of observers during his stint with Southampton and Manchester City during which time he won 46 caps for England. Channon had apparently liked horses and horseracing a much as he liked football and footballers. What Channon never expected was that he would not only make a career training horses, he would become one of the best with 200 horses in his care. "People ask me why I turned my back on football," Channon said. "It's more truthful to say that football gave me up." It has been a long, hard and enjoyable race for Channon from a council house on Salisbury Plain to become master of one of the last great private training establishments in the country at West Ilsley bought from the Queen in 1999 after he quit his stables at Lambourn amid some of the best known members of the racing fraternity.

Channon briefly looked for a job in football after he finished playing. "I once tried for the manager's job at Wolves, but they asked me to be head coach instead. I didn't fancy a manager coming and not wanting me. I couldn't see it working. Old age is a bastard. My playing days were over, I had time on my hands and I knew I had to get off my backside. I stumbled into racing because I had nothing else to do. It was suggested I had a go at training and it started off as a hobby. It took off and became my living and my joy. I never imagined it would lead to this." Channon is among a distinguished group of thoroughbred footballers who made a happy career switch.

Francis Lee, from Channon's former club Manchester City, was a successful trainer. Channon's owners include Alan Ball a close friend from his playing days and there is another well-known breeder in Kevin Keegan. Niall Quinn, the former Republic of Ireland striker, has a keen interest in racing and has links with horses through his Dublin business connections. Sir Alex Ferguson had a profitable share in Rock of Gibraltar, talented winner of the 2000 guineas in 2002 and later made investments in other promising colts and fillies. It remains interesting to conjecture how much the row over shares and bloodstock rights of Gibraltar led to the sale of huge shareholdings in United and the eventual vulnerability to the take-over by the Glazers.

A footballers' brain and instinct, it seems, can be applied to judging the potential and training of horses. It might have been a football manager talking rather than a racehorse trainer when Channon summed up his work ethic: "I do my best with the cards I'm given. My horses are not here for fun. They are fit and hardy, not wimps, and there's no hiding place for them on the gallops or the racecourse." There's something of the footballer lingering inside another Channon racing philosophy: "I've never been frightened to have a go against the best. If there's a chink in their armour my horses will find it." Racing did not take kindly to Channon initially, rejecting his first application to become a trainer. Channon, who won an F.A. Cup winner's medal when Southampton beat Manchester United in 1976, became the first footballer to take racing by storm. He is unlikely to be the last.

TV TRANSFERS

It is easy to overlook some of the more modern sporting acrobats who made the considerable leap from playing football to the less physically exerting but more mentally taxing task of talking about it on screen. It seemed unlikely that Gary Lineker would ever transfer his skill and precision *in* the box with Leicester City, Everton, Barcelona and Spurs, to a nonchalance *on* it. The superbly aplomb Des Lynam looked irreplaceable until Lineker took his chair on Match of the Day, adding the touch of authority that comes from playing 80 games for England. The demands of live TV are not to be underestimated with its collection of notorious double entendres involving the top pros of the screen... "dipping their cox in the water" etc. Lineker happily laughed off his "race-boat day" gaffe when working for Football Focus and his rather more spectacular faux pas during his first appearance as a fledgling broadcaster in 1996.

"I was reporting for ITV in France at a Manchester United European tie. I was still playing at the time and they sent me on to the pitch. I said something like 'It's quite firm out here. All the players will be wearing rubbers tonight.' I could hear people sniggering in my ear and I could not work out why. I was wooden and just learning a new trade. I would not like to look back at those programmes now. I was obviously not bad enough for them to kick me out." He added the obvious: "I'm comfortable now. I know how it works." He knew the TV game so well in fact that he was twice named Royal Television Society Sports Presenter of the Year. Lineker was well prepared for the hidden pitfalls from references to golf balls when he took his charm and broadcasting nous into the world of the Royal and Ancient as successor to Steve Rider as the new face of television golf on the BBC.

He was beside the 18th at the Old Course in 1995 when Costantino Rocca holed the fabulous putt to tie The Open with John Daly. He was in at the death at Carnoustie in 1999 when Jean Van de Velde lost it and he was among the fans on the 18th green at Muirfield in 1992 when Nick Faldo holed the winning putt. Golf had taken a back seat when Lineker played his football but he began playing more earnestly during a stint of football in Japan. He became hooked (apologies) on golf and sold his London home to take a house next to the course at Sunningdale where he became a low handicap player following in the divots of his grandfather who played off four. Lineker's affability, modesty and friendly demeanour were harnessed to make a highly successful career on the box after his scoring dynamics in the box.

Andy Gray, also a former Everton striker, joined the likes of Alan Hansen, and Mark Lawrenson, in making a smooth transition from player to pundit. Gray's passion for the game and his honesty make him compulsive viewing, his confidence seemingly growing as quickly as his hair vanished mocking the chant of Dundee United supporters before he joined Villa and Wolves on his way to Everton, "Who's the boy with the golden hair?". Not that his voice could ever be said to have golden qualities. More likely there is a hint of truth in the story that Mel Gibson modelled his Scottish accent on Gray's for the part of William Wallace in the film Braveheart. Gray joined Sky Sports on day one with presenter Richard Keys, whose claim to fame in the Manchester media section before he took his star role with Sky, was a humorous impersonation of John Bond, then manager of Manchester City.

Gray has never sat on the fence where so many pundits were prepared to roost. For example the Scot voiced strong opinions on the question of the manager of England, Sven Goran Eriksson, that Englishmen may have felt but were not prepared to express publically for fear of being charged with soccer treason. "I am against him both as a foreigner and as someone not good enough," he said in one interview on reaching his 50th birthday before England took part in the 2006 World Cup finals. "I don't think England need a foreign coach. None of the major countries have one. Any Englishman could have done as well with the players he's had at his disposal for the last six years. He has underachieved. I have not seen him do anything to influence a game when it really mattered. I could manage England and win as many games. There is so much talent available. If England had Fergie, Wenger or Mourinho (conveniently overlooking his 'foreigner' theory!) in charge, they would win the World Cup in Germany."

Gray also has interesting views on club management. "There was an era when Kenny Dalglish and Graeme Souness stepped out of having highly successful careers as players into management at the highest level. There is much less of that now. I don't see Alan Shearer or Roy Keane going straight into a big job." Gray survived in the industry thanks to his willingness to learn from television pros unlike some former sportspeople who either do not consider they were in need of an apprenticeship, or were unable to grasp the basics of, say, interview technique when tutored by journalists. "Football speak" was quickly booted out of him, so to speak.

Sir Trevor Brooking, the former West Ham playmaker and a safe pair of hands in any company, gave up the comfort zone of the BBC commentary box, to spearhead the F.A.'s neglected drive to find and develop the talent that slipped through the nets of club and country. His position of development director thrust upon him the responsibilities of developing a coaching blueprint especially at youth level. "I used to run a small football academy in Brentwood and I would complain and moan about the technical ability of the kids. I could see an annual decline in the skill factor. So I was delighted to take the chance to do something about it. I could see the lack of coaching quality and the general demise of school sports. We must be grateful to the mums and dads who run junior teams. But those kids could not improve without proper coaching."

Brooking was not alone in decrying the declining numbers of English players in the Premiership where 60 percent were foreign as the game moved at a questionable pace into the twenty first century. "The clubs, some of whom have overseas players coming through the system, can't be blamed," Brooking pointed out. "The message is that the technical quality of English youngsters isn't good enough. Reaching children by the age of nine is too late. We need quality coaching for the six to nine-year-old age group."

DOTING DADS

IT WAS HARRY GOODWIN of Manchester City who I first heard talk about the "Doting Dads." It could, I suppose, have been any other soccer scout ushering young players into a club's junior academies and being offered a chance to set foot on the bottom rung of the slippery football ladder. How many youngsters were hampered, ruined even, by Dads who saw themselves in the colours of their favourite team. "Go for it son… get stuck in," they would bellow from the touchline when wise heads were looking for other less obvious qualities, realising that a youngster's development depends so much on qualities outside the ability to play football like temperament, pace, stamina, courage, physically as well as mentally, unselfishness and outright selfishness. The danger of over-coaching can never be ignored. There were Mollycoddling Mums, too, shrieking from the touchline often willing to invade the pitch wielding an umbrella to protect their precious infant prodigy from some bullying monster.

"You see some parents intimidating their kids, so we would like to keep them in a roped-off area where they can watch their kids, but they are kept away from the game," Sir Trevor Brooking, Development director at the F.A. was moved to say many years after the Godwin observation. Cissie Charlton, with her footballing heritage in Ashington and a hard life among mining folk, had a master's degree in management and encouragement of outstanding talent. To be mother to two of the most famous brothers in the history of the game made her feel a proud and privileged wife of a pit worker.

One son, Jack, born on 8th. May, 1935, was the ugly duckling footballer. The other, Bobby, born on 11th. October, 1937, the swan. But both respected their gifts, and worked hard to improve them. Jack played a record 773 games for Leeds United, scoring 96 times, some as an orthodox striker; Bobby's total of games with Manchester United was 752 (2 as sub) with 247 goals to his name representing a strike rate of a goal every three games. The Charltons won 20 of the 28 internationals they played together climaxed by success in the World Cup, drawing six and losing just two – a winning percentage of 71.4. Jack was outgoing; Bobby more introverted. But both, in their own ways, had a communicator's touch. That was particularly evident when Bobby, myself and another journalist, David Meek of the *Manchester Evening News*, became separated from the main United contingent in Berlin afer a game against Hertha.

The group happily accepted an invitation to be guests in the Officers' Mess at RAF Gatow. Bobby, David and myself missed the party bus to the RAF station and went by taxi. "Let's go to the Sergeants' Mess instead," ventured Bobby, a soldier during his National Service, as we reported to the Guard Room. It was a conscious social and democratic suggestion that brought joy to the mess members and the unexpected trio of Mancunian visitors. Ever the diplomat, Bobby charmed and entertained the assembled NCOs only to be cleverly thwarted by the Mess President when he attempted to pay for a round and return the generous hospitality. "Thank you Bobby," said the MP, "but the rule here tonight is that honoured guests pay at the exchange rate of a penny to the German mark." The wonderful evening cost us a few pence each!

Proud mums and "doting" dads have supplied many instances of footballing progeny. Manchester United had the Greenhoffs, Brian and Jimmy, and the Nevilles Gary and Phil, and Jack Rowley, my idol and later team-mate in Showbiz games and Arthur, a record marksman mainly with Leicester City and Fulham, are random examples of family talent. The gene factor in football does not end there. Three Wallace brothers Danny, Rodney and Ray played in the same Southampton League team 24 times until September 1989. It was the first time for 65 years that three brothers had appeared together in a First Division team.

Middlesbrough had the Carr brothers in 1920, three

Tonners turned out for Clapton Orient in season 1919-20 and the trio of Jacks, David, Donald and Jack, were aces for Plymouth Argyle in 1920. Identical or similar twins gave referees headches, too. There were Rodney and Ray Wallace, David and Peter Jackson, and the Morgans Ian and Roger of QPR. West Brom's Adam and James Chambers, then 18, were the first twins to represent England against Cameroon in the World Youth Championship, and later teamed up at club level. Just to add to the confusions of footballing family trees, Alex Herd (at 39) and David (just 17) made the first father and son duo in League football when they played for Stockport County in May, 1951. The Bowyers took over the baton 39 years later when player manager Bowyer (39) and Gary (18) both turned out for Hereford United at Scunthorpe United. Manager George Eastham Snr. and his son George Jnr. were inside forward partners for Ards in the Irish League in 1954-55. Parental loyalties were stretched to the limit in the Kelly family. Alan Kelly (21) kept goal for Peston North End against Bury, whose custodian was Gary (23). Their dad, Alan Kelly Snr. who was between the sticks for Preston in the 1964 F.A. Cup Final and won 47 caps for the Republic of Ireland, flew from the USA to watch the sons he instructed in the teasing ramifications of goalkeepking, on opposite sides. Preston won 2-1 at Bury on January 13, 1990.

Father and son were champs, too. John Aston Snr. won a Championship medal with Manchester United in 1952 and John Jnr. did likewise in 1967 as a left winger. John Snr, a successful convert from forward to left back who spearheaded United's coaching staff for some years, was fiercely loyal to his club. One Sunday having become involved in a heated argument over a lunchtime pint, Aston senior left the pub, returning in his best suit so that he could be considered "properly dressed" should the discussion escalate into a physical confrontation.

ALL ROUNDERS

DEBATE HAS RAGED since day one of soccer history about who was the the game's most versatile player. Shankly believed Sir Tom Finney was the most rounded player of all, insisting that despite his lack of height he had the skill and football know-how to even play at centre half. Many believed that John Charles was versatility personified playing with equal effectiveness as striker or centre half without ever needing to resort to over-evident use of his immensely strong physique. To many fans in England, Wales and Italy, Charles was "King Charles" or the "Gentle Giant."

There have been so many all-rounders in a wide range of sports. My idol Denis Compton won caps at soccer and cricket for England, paying 158 games for Arsenal, often with his brother, Les, the Middlesex wicket-keeper, and scored 90 goals. He also won wartime League and Cup honours while Leslie won two full caps in 1951 with Arsenal. Runs flowed from the Compton willow: 38,942 runs in all (5,807 in Tests) including 123 first-class centuries and he was also the youngest Englishman to reach a ton in his first Test against Australia in 1938.

Despite the demands of becoming a doctor of medicine, Dr. Kevin O'Flanagan of Dublin also found the time to develop his skill at soccer, scoring on his debut for Arsenal. He won three soccer caps. It must have been to the consternation of his friends that the doctor was also a multi-capped Irish rugby player. The success in sport doesn't end there. Dr. O'Flanagan was also a champion of Ireland in track and field events. And just to rub salt into the permanent injuries of the sport-challenged masses, he excelled at golf and tennis.

The talents of Stanley Harris were wide-ranging. Stanley turned down the chance of joining the team for the 1920 Olympics to concentrate on rugby and toured South Africa with the Lions four years later and stayed there for a time winning the amateur boxing lightweight championship and playing for South Africa in the Davis Cup. Later back in England he won the All-England mixed doubles and played water polo for England. A neighbour Gordon Willmott provided the fascinating insight that during World War One, Harris was a gunnery officer and just to add insult to injury for those blessed with two left feet, he took up the unlikely diversion of ballroom dancing while recovering from his war wounds. No surprise, then, that Mr. Harris hit the target and reached the finals of the World Championships! A revered local hero was Walter Jones, a bank official, who was a dashing centre forward for Altrincham in the Cheshire League, played rugby with Rochdale Hornets, cricket in the Lancashire League and bowled, on a green, that is, to county standard. He was an icon then to many teenagers, unexposed to the later temptations to come from television, thus reducing involvement in sport during the formative years.

"Normal" folk are entitled to ask how it is that genes

do so generously bestow such a wide variety of skills and qualities on one person. Charles Burgess ("CB") Fry was blessed with a share that enabled him to excel in a range of sports as well as take his place in the field of academics. To anyone of average skills or brain capacity, his versatility was mind blowing. The son of Croydon (born 1872) scored almost 40,000 first-class runs, averaging 50.22 and played for England 26 times and was captain in six Tests. CB peaked in 1901 scoring 3,417 runs including centuries in six successive innings. He excelled at soccer, of course, playing for England and was a member of the Southampton team beaten 2-1 by Sheffield United in the 1902 Cup Final at Crystal Palace. Extra time would not have stretched CB athletically, of course. In 1893 he set a new world long-jump record at 23ft. 6and a half inches at Oxford's Iffley Road where Roger Bannister, also a medical doctor, thrilled a huge audience in 1954 by breaking the four-minute barrier for the mile. CB, thankfully, had a memory weakness, apparently not realising that the Olympic Games were taking place in 1896. His Oxford leap would have won a gold medal with three feet to spare! CB, of course, played rugby for Blackheath, a giant club then, and for the Barbarians. He was also a journalist, taught at Charterhouse, was a Naval commander and stood for parliament three times. An offer of the throne of the Kingdom of Albania was declined – in politically correct terms, of course.

After playing cricket with Somerset and touring with the British Lions in the late-19th. century, Arthur Paul switched his sporting talents to soccer, playing in goal for Blackburn Rovers. Ken Jones (same name as a famous sporting journalist many years later) won a then record 44 caps for Wales as a wing in the Forties and Fifties and used his formidable pace to win an Olympic silver in the British 4x100 relay team at the London Olympics in 1948.

GOLDEN OLDIES

I FEEL FORTUNATE to have stood on the terraces and reported on matches in the golden age of football and footballers. Clubs since have launched huge financial operations with varying success, usually short-term in duration and rarely visionary in the planning. Fitness routines were old hat by modern standards with most teams finely tuned and athletically prepared. But back then it used to be not uncommon for a local hero to be spotted in some hostelry near the ground not too far from kick-off time and certainly in there afterwards holding court. Yet from the weekly visits to Maine Road (Old Trafford was a shambles, devastated by German bombs) a fan of United one week, City the next, there was an abundance of players to drool over. And there was always the Beswick Prize Silver Band, or the "Besses," meat pies and Eccles cakes as delightful additional attractions.

Players took opponents on and dribbled past knowing that they would (usually) not be the victim of a scything challenge. They made defence-splitting passes, rarely passed back to the goalkeeper except under extreme pressure and never, or very rarely, feigned injury yet controlled a sodden leather ball on mud skidpans with nonchalant ease. Goals abounded it seemed and 0–0 tactical stalemates were rare, though of course there have been classic goalless draws.

It is unlikely that there will be many repeats of the 6-6 draw between Leicester City and Arsenal on April 21, 1930, Arsenal's David Halliday netting four times. Another 6-6 thriller featured a hat-trick for Middlesbrough by Brian Clough, when it was goals that did his talking. Pass the smelling salts! Though some cute historian or statistician will lurk with a counter claim, those two bonanza games were, I believe, the only times drawn games in the Football League have been so extravagantly endowed with goals, though we can all recall games when the score should have been at least 7-7!

More recently, two Belgian teams went on a goal scoring binge, again scoring six each. Branko Strupar smashed a hat-trick of penalties for Racing Genk while Toni Brogno scored four for Westerlo in August, 1999. Feelings, understandably, ran high on the pitch with each team having two players dismissed. It was a hot-blooded day in March, 2000, when Gimnasia y Esgrima de La Plata (a nightmare mouthful for commentators!) and Colon de Santa Fe (that's better) shared 12 goals in the Argentine League.

And of course Arbroath went on a record rampage and beat Bon Accord of Aberdeen 36-0 in a first round Scottish Cup tie in 1885 – one John Petrie netting 13 goals - although often forgotten is the fact that on the same day in the same competition Dundee beat Aberdeen Rovers 35-0. Not a good day for Aberdeen!

Joe Payne lived up to his name at Bristol Rovers in the old Div Three (South) hammering ten of Luton Town's goals in April 1936. William Ralph Dean – or

Dixie to Everton fans – was somewhat prolific, netting 60 goals in 39 First Division games in season 1927-28. Dixie also scored three times in the F.A. Cup and a further 19 in representative games for a grand total of 82 in a free-scoring season.

The ascendancy of defence over attack – or were strikers less effective? – is neatly illustrated by Alan Shearer's exploits for Blackburn Rovers where he became the first player since World War Two to top 30 goals in three successive seasons; 31, 34, 31 from season 1993-4. David Halliday went one season better with Sunderland with hauls of 38, 36, 36 and 49 but that was back in the twenties. It was a personal observation that so many of the best players, especially centre forwards, it seemed, had wavy hair, though the advent of "baldies" around the turn of the century changed that cherished image.

From the forties to the seventies at least, inside forwards, wingers and goalkeepers of stature not to mention strikers could be seen in abundance. It is difficult to understand the current fad of passing back to a goalkeeper with other options available, considering that it takes much less than average football intelligence to note that possession is lost, probably nine times out of ten, once the goalkeeper balloons the ball upfield. So much for possession being nine-tenths of football law. But we always knew that the manager's indecision was final! They do change their minds as well as their allegiance.

Sir Alex Ferguson announced his retirement after his contract expired in 2002, but three months before he was due to walk out of Old Trafford for good, he signed a new three-year deal. There was the about-face by Ron Atkinson, two days after declaring he had the best job in the game at Sheffield Wednesday, he switched to Aston Villa. Steve McMahon went right to the wire at Blackpool with the club revealing he had quit. Then the former Liverpool mid-fielder turned up at the end of the press conference called to announce his departure, to seek a meeting with the club chairman Carl Oyston. He wanted to withdraw his resignation – not that he ever withdrew from any tackle in a successful career that climaxed at Liverpool. Not all returns had a happy ending.

The most emotional "comeback" by far was Denis Law's return to Old Trafford nine months after he revisited Maine Road in 1973. Not only did his goal apply another relegation nail to United, Law's goal was in the outrageous class – a backheeler taken with a sense of inevitability and decidedly mixed emotions. It wasn't that easy for Sol Campbell when he returned to White Hart Lane in 2001 with Tottenham's arch rivals Arsenal. Sol was obliged to endure a barrier of hate and insults from Spurs' fans as he ran out on to the pitch. West Ham fans had to wait for five years until 1994 before they could publically inform Paul Ince what they thought of him following his defection to Manchester United.

Pat Jennings' return to White Hart Lane had a double-edged barb for the Spurs' fans who saw their goalkeeper idol defect to Arsenal for £45,000. A year later Jennings, capped a record 119 times by Northern Ireland, was back, kept a clean sheet – and Arsenal won

5-0. It seemed Bobby Moore was a fixture at West Ham where he spent 16 glorious years until he was allowed to move on to Fulham. Bobby's new club crashed 2-0 in the 1975 F.A. Cup Final at Wembley, thus robbing Moore of a second gong to add to his winners' medal with West Ham 11 years earlier.

Players, it seems, care less about allegiance than besotted fans, understandably exercising the theoretical right of every citizen to take his talents to a workplace of his choice at the invitation of an employer. Manchester had more than its share of "litmus" transfers, unlike supporters who "would not be seen dead" in such-and-such-a-shirt. Peter Swales, City's ever-optimistic chairman and a blue from birth, banned red furnishings from his household and frowned on a boyfriend of one of his daughters who was a confessed United fan. Law became blue, turned to red and with another shot of alkali turned blue again; a colourful player in more ways than one. After City came Torino and then United in 1961 where Law swashbuckled through a decade of arm-raised goal glory with 171 goals in 309 League games. In 1973 Law was back in the blue room. Injury finally forced him to rest his battered body aged 33.

Who else but Law and Manchester City could experience this mind-blowing statistic in the F.A. Cup. "Who scored all six goals in a tie and finished on the losing side?" That tasty quiz teaser could legitimately be extended to seven goals. With City coasting 6-2 against Luton Town in a fourth round tie in 1961, the game was abandoned after 69 minutes because the pitch became waterlogged. Yes, City lost the re-run 3-1. And of course

Law scored City's goal, his seventh of the "tie."

Blue-red dealing had begun long before Law. Way back in 1906, Billy Meredith, the wonder Welsh winger, upped pulse rates by leaving Maine Road and joining United. But 15 years later – a career span in itself – the star, who played with a toothpick in his mouth, became a Blue again when well into his forties, eventually retiring days short of his 50th birthday to rival Stan Matthews for longevity in the game. Peter Barnes, son of Ken, a distinguished wing half at Maine Road in the 50s, went to West Brom and was then signed by Ron Atkinson in 1985 for a successful two-year stint at Old Trafford and then returned to the ground where he first watched matches sitting on his mother's knee. Sammy McIlroy, the last of the famous Babes produced in the Busby reign who became a favourite with fans of Northern Ireland, winning 55 caps in 15 distinguished years, also savoured the litmus treatment. Brian Kidd, too, joined the Red-Blue club. Still in his teens, Kidd was part of the team that finally realised Sir Matt Busby's European Cup dream in 1968. Then after joining Arsenal in 1974, the Kidd from Collyhurst, a partisan suburb of Manchester, became a Blue two years later and made it a happy return home with City, plundering 44 goals in 97 games. So, not surprisingly, few heads were turned heads when Stuart Pearce, latest in the long parade of City managers, made his move to sign ex-United striker Andy Cole, in his first full season at the helm of an always interesting ship rarely sailing in calm waters.

Blue-red tinges are not restricted to players and fans. Sidney Rose, a director of Manchester City, had a secret affinity with Manchester United and unknown to his fellow directors at Maine Road, he skipped the City match and took to the road to watch United in a Cup semi-final at Hillsborough. The journey went well and with Hillsborough almost in sight and not a sign of a traffic snarl-up, Sidney turned to his son and said: "Did we bring the piano?" "The piano?" echoed his son. "Yes, the piano," replied Sidney with the calm befitting an eminent surgeon. "I left the tickets on top of it."

NEW BEGINNINGS

LIFE IN SPORT can begin or at least continue at 40. Steve Davis, the de-throned king of snooker, took an amble down "amnesia avenue" when he reached the final of the UK snooker championship at 48 bidding to undercut the oldest winner of the title, Doug Mountjoy, at two years younger. It was little consolation for sporting veterans and ever-hopefuls that Ding Junhui, the boy wonder from China, aged just 18, whipped him 10-6 in the final. Evergreen golfers have the consolation that Jack Nicklaus grabbed his sixth US Masters title at Augusta in 1986 aged 46. And that was six years after the leading tournament topper last won a major.

Those with pugilistic inclinations will have noted that George Foreman regained the title aged 45 by beating Michael Moorer, 20 years after the Punching Preacher lost his world heavyweight title belt to Muhammad Ali in the "Rumble in the Jungle" in 1974. Tennis buffs will have noted that Martina Navratilova made a comeback into the singles game in 2004 aged 47. That was more than ten years since she last competed on her own in a career that saw her snaffle 167 singles titles (repeat 167) including nine at Wimbledon and four US Opens. New balls please.

Cricket at club level has always had its veterans like Wilf Laidlaw at Timperley in Cheshire who played until he was almost 80. Another more aggressive and successful off-spinner Fred Titmus played his last game for Middlesex at the ripe old cricket age of 50 in 1982. Titmus was a toddler of 42 when he played his last of 53 Tests in 1975; another highlight in a sporting life that spanned five decades.

Those with high ambitions and low achievements in sport, are entitled to chuckle (well almost) at the failure of the Masters of Sport. It was no joke for punters strolling to the pay-out window when jockey Roger Loughran, about to grab his first win as a pro in 2005, celebrated too soon at Leopardstown, punched the air in triumph mistaking the positioning of the winning post and finished third. Another major racing upset was not the jockey's fault when Devon Loch bellyflopped when a clear leader with just 40 yards remaining of the 1956 Grand National, surrendering the crown to ESB. We've often heard the excuse "that's football" after a crunch defeat. This time Devon Loch's owner, the Queen Mother, was equally philosophical. "That's horse racing," she said.

We humans are always making mistakes, but those of the stars of sport are captured on camera for posterity. Stuart Pearce, Gareth Southgate and David Beckham all ballooned penalty kicks at vital times to kindly reassure novice players. Robert Pires wasn't falling into the "balloon" trap when he took a spot kick for Arsenal against Manchester City. Pires passed the buck so to speak, side-stepping the ball to Thierry Henry, which he was perfectly entitled to do if he cared, only for his team-mate to miss. "People forget soccer is entertainment," Henry explained later. Pires should have explained the joke to his team-mate.

Rugby players can miss vital kicks too. Don Fox had an easy kick to win the League's Challenge Cup in 1968. Wakefield were 11-10 in arrears against Leeds in soaking conditions. Fox squirted his shot wide of the target and held his hands. Commentator Eddie Waring uttered the well-remembered line: "He's missed it... the poor lad." Rene Higuita, the eccentric Columbian goalkeeper, "lost" it when he tried to enliven a mundane 1990 World Cup by dribbling well out of his goal in a second round tie against Cameroon. He lost the ball to the mercurial Roger Milla who dashed off and had the indecency to score his second which confirmed a shock 2-1 success.

Maths can hit the unwary sportsman. Caddie Miles Byrne discovered he had bagged an extra driver which would cost Ian Woosnam two shots when the battling little Welshman was fighting for the lead on the final day of The Open in 2001. "You're going to go ballistic," Byrne admitted. Woosnam did – and sacked him two weeks later when he overslept and missed tee-off time at the Scandanavian Open. Shaun Pollock miscalculated, too. He told Mark Boucher he needed only to block the final ball against Sri Lanka in the Group stages of the 2003 World Cup. But Shaun had missed the point, miscalculating the complex Duckworth–Lewis system and South Africa went out as did Pollock as captain soon afterwards. An athletic slip by humans cost the US a gold in the Athens Olympics in 2004. Afer looking unbeatable in qualifying, the US women's 4x100m relay team blew it when Lauryn Williams started off too soon for Marion Jones to hand her the baton. Jamaicia "won" gold in a slower time than the US had clocked in qualifying.

Personal sporting catastrophies don't come much bigger than the blunder that cost Frenchman Jean Van de Velde the 1999 Open trophy at Carnoustie. Jean needed just a six at the par-four last to win golf's grand prix. But his second shot hit the grandstand and even worse his next went into the Barry Burn. After accepting a penalty drop, Jean took off his shoes and socks and went into the water. His seven still won him a play-off but his major chance had come and gone in a splash.

COLLEAGUES

LAUGHTER LINES

SPORT OF ANY variety seems to induce humour among its competitors and wordsmiths. Seemingly by tradition, the media always found a suitable premises (licensed of course) as an informal HQ and rendezvous point when covering assignments abroad. One such place was a bar-restaurant converted from a synagogue near Manchester United's team hotel in Prague. "What do we call this gaff then?" queried one reporter. Paddy Barclay, then of *The Guardian*, seemed hardly to think before he replied: "The bar-mitsfa, of course."

Malcolm Broadie, of the *Belfast Telegraph*, was, quite understandably, on a high when he filed his report of Northern Ireland's quite magnificent if slender victory over host country Spain in Valencia during the 1982 WC finals. "Magnifico...magnifico...magnifico..." he dictated his joyous report to a copytaker. "Okay, Malcolm," she replied in an indifferent tone, "I heard you first time." Before high-tech and after pigeon copy carriers and cables, reporters dictated their stories from phone box, press box, bar, private house or any available telephone link. It so often seemed that the typist and reporter were invariably struggling with inferior quality sound or one-way telephone lines. It never helped, either, to be asked by the copytaker after every paragraph, "is there much more of this," indicating that he or she believed you had over-written.

Most telephonists were excellent typists; a small number either bored or indifferent. One I knew had trouble spelling "half time" early in the day, but later in the evening after a glass or two of refreshment, would purr, "Normal spelling?" when you were prepared to spell out phonetically some unpronounceable foreign name.

It was after that triumph against Spain thanks to Gerry Armstrong's super goal that I probably saved one member of the Northern Ireland contingent from an embarrassing "own goal" (if not gaol). Team manager Billy Bingham gave the players a weekend to relax before moving to Madrid for the later stages of the tournament. A red-haired full back, who served Manchester United with distinction, swerved towards me from the celebrations wearing only a pair of baggy shorts and a broad grin. A clutch of Spanish fans, mainly of female gender, were walking behind him unknown to Jimmy Nicholl. Nor was he aware that two members of the Guarda Civil on motorbikes were turning off the main road in his direction. Jimmy was about to display his joy and a good deal of his manhood to the world with an uninhibited "mooning" when I yelled: "Man on Jimmy!" Shorts rapidly hoisted, Jimmy walked on without a glance in any direction. The Guarda drove by, Jimmy bought me a large one later.

Managers and players, like readers, have no knowledge of the pitfalls and problems, expected and unexpected, that taunted the reporter before improved communications and technology took over to make part of the job a little easier. 'Wee' Jimmy Dubois joined his colleagues and a sprinkling of players after a Northern Ireland game in Sofia, where communications were to say the least erratic. Everybody had filed, apart from Jimmy whose edition time for the *Belfast Newsletter* was much in advance of the norm. A sheaf of notes prepared for dictation of his lengthy despatch were clutched in Jimmy's hand as he awaited his telephone call. Allan Hunter, a big central defender from Ipswich, unaware that Jimmy had yet to file, grabbed the sheaf of notes and tossed it out of the window into the icy Bulgarian night. Dubois, a teammate of Harry Gregg in their days as junior footballers in Belfast, turned as white as the snowflakes. Only then did Hunter realise the seriousness of his innocent jape. Hunter was on his feet and vanished in a flash, returning minutes later with every page of the 1,000 word missive intact to be later telephoned to Belfast without a further hitch.. "Never seen Big Allan move as fast," muttered a much relieved correspondent of the *Belfast Newsletter*.

Another fascinating memory of covering Northern Ireland football came during an important fixture in Vienna against Austria. The Birmingham Symphony Orchestra, then under the commanding baton of Simon Rattle, were in town and I and another journalist went to the orchestra's hotel the evening before the match to try and meet some of the musicians. We did, particularly members of the brass section, who all seemed to have been recruited from Yorkshire bands, and several soccer-interested string players. We discovered that many of the musicians had been trying to locate and meet the footballers, so we issued invitations with Billy Bingham's approval for a get-together after the match the following night. A memorable mix of wine, music and sociability went with a convivial swing until one particularly handsome member of Bingham's strike force took a fancy to an attractive female first violin. "Handsome Striker" had no idea that first violin's fiance was also at the party and before a serious discordant note could be struck, the last waltz, so to speak, was played.

McNAMARA'S BAND

The career of Desmond Hackett, a dashing columnist of the *Daily Express* in its most exciting years, was never less than extravagantly colourful. Revised flight times, other disruptions to his travel plans and most significantly of all being whisked through several different time zones on the journey to Tokyo for the Olympics in 1964 when travel lacked the pace of later years, promoted a memorable first dispatch. "I know who I am," filed Hackett. "I know where I am. But I don't know what day of the week it is." That was the beginning of a somewhat unorthodox Olympics for Hackett alongside such Fleet Street giants, and formidable rivals, as Peter Wilson (*Daily Mirror*), J.L. Manning (*Daily Mail*) and Sam Leitch (*Sunday Mirror*).

An "unknown" London wrestler unexpectedly defeated a famous Japanese wrestler Saito (one of the hosts greatest hopes for gold) when eyes were focussed in other directions. The crowd in the wrestling arena, that included Emperor Hirohito, were dumbstruck and Saito had his pigtail ceremonially hacked off after the bout.

When Hackett learned that the English wrestler, Denis McNamara, was a police sergeant in the East End, his creative imagination went into overdrive. A colleague in London was summoned to find Sgt. McNamara's service number. An *Express* sub editor John Lloyd, who had been despatched to Japan to give Hackett any back-up he might require, was on hand. With less exposure on TV and a less pacey infiltration of happenings outside the mainstream of events, Hackett's "leg man" was sent on an urgent mission. "Find out about McNamara – rapido," Lloyd was urged. He did exactly that with the help of a colleague in London at great speed and in considerable detail and Hackett, entirely based on second hand information, wrote a memorable piece headlined "McNamara's Band" in a shameless and colourful parody.

Hackett urgently summoned the aide of his assistant in writing a follow up to the popular Gold triumph of Anne Packer in the 400 metres; a success made all the more poignant by the subsequent fate of her finance Robbie Brightwell in the 200 metres, where he snatched only a Silver, thus devaluing a heart-tugging story of a double Olympic Gold triumph by the young sweethearts. Lloyd hired a cycle to race to the Olympic Village with the mid-evening curfew rapidly approaching. Brightwell was "in hiding". But with the help of fellow-Welshman Lyn "The Leap" Davies, whose long-jumping had been a sensation also topped by Gold, Lloyd was escorted to Brightwell's room. Brightwell, captain of the squad, unzipped his training bag and there glinting within was with the brightness of a diamond in the sunlight, was Anne Packer's gold medal, "given to my darling as a present to start our married life."

"What a girl," exclaimed Brightwell – and promptly burst into tears unaware that he had a media presence. Brightwell must have known that his plea not to reveal his emotional outburst would go unheeded.

"Great work John, get back here as quickly as you can," urged Hackett.

"What about the bike?" queried Lloyd by now with the curfew passed, rated as an unwelcome intruder in the village.

"To hell with that – grab a cab, steal a car – just get back here," ordered Hackett who enjoyed wrenching every tear out of a red-hot human interest story in his urgent dispatch from the detail again supplied second hand. A Brightwell off-spring Ian, blessed with pace of course, later made his mark as a footballer at Manchester City.

Hackett, of course, applied a policy of damage limitation on any assignment and assumed exclusive charge of the telephone designated to the *Daily Express* on one visit to the San Siro stadium, Milan. Potter, then a rookie reporter outside the UK, implored a friendly Italian journalist to allow him the use of his phone, making "collect" calls through the international switchboard to his office in Manchester. Hackett did not receive one call from his office; mine never stopped ringing as if to underline the question of morality and teamwork!

FUN AND CHEERS

JOURNALISTS, THE LAW and medics have always shared a liking for liquor. One former colleague in Belfast used to begin his mid-day drink by ordering two pints of Guinness and a large gin and tonic. Then he would turn to his companions and inquire: "Now what are you boys having." A colleague of his of less than average height, reputedly took a drink or two late on a Saturday night after finishing his shift and before catching the last train home out of Belfast. In order to guarantee his safety when he alighted at the station halt with its deep step to the platform, he used to ensure that the porter was never short of a packet of 20. One Saturday the nicely mellowed hack put out his hand expecting the protective arm of the friendly porter only to plunge several feet on to the platform. The porter had failed to explain that it was his night off. The injuries were more to the reporter's pride than to his body.

A delightfully Irish story involved four journalists from Dublin driving back to the city late at night after covering a game in Cork. They stopped a Garda in a dimly lit little town some way south of Dublin and inquired, "Officer, do you know where four decent Dublin boys can get a drink in this little town at this time of night?"

"No, sur," replied the Garda, "I don't... but I know where five can," as he clambered into the back seat of the car.

Geoffrey Green of *The Times* was never reluctant to take a drink at work or at play, yet his accuracy was unequalled and his prose enviable. He was one of the favourites of Bill Shankly (a teetotaller who did take the occasional dram on doctor's orders) presumably because he had experience as a highly respected amateur centre. Geoffrey, with incredible good fortune, once escaped arrest as he walked along a line of troops guarding the concourse on arrival at an Eastern Bloc airport, "inspecting" the armed guard with a royal flourish. Geoffrey used to enjoy telling of his first meeting with the new England cap, Bobby Charlton. A party was in full swing at a bar atop the team's hotel. Charlton was engaged in performing double forward rolls, narrowly failing in his attempts to end the acrobatic manoeuvre with his head lodged in a Cossack hat across the room.

"Next time I was with England climbing up the steps on to the aircraft, I felt a tap on my shoulder and it was Bobby," recalled Green, still fascinated by Charlton's acrobatic determination. "I can do it now," he said. They became close friends. Green was a trouper; sociable, friendly and ever-helpful. He once singed my hair with a burning newspaper proffered when the press box lights and the floodlights, as they always seemed to do then, went out in the middle of dictating an overdue re-write.

The Express in Manchester had a sub-editor with a photographic brain, particularly in relation to athletics and boxing. No question, even if deviously couched, would throw Bryn Davies out of his stride; be it times, dates or personal bests. Even after a joust with Guinness during his mid-shift break, Bryn remained utterly reliable if a little more effusive, on one occasion pushing who he thought was a friend in the back while he used the urinal only to discover later that it was the new editor on his first day in charge. Even when drink became a problem, Bryn never forgot his facts and figures. He was given leave of absence to recover and was eventually paraded before a psychiatrist who in kindly terms offered his expert advice on how to reorganise his life without recourse to alcohol. "I don't need a medic to tell me how to achieve that," Davies insisted. He discharged himself from medical care and triumphed unaided and became an abstainer – only to sadly die from a heart attack some five years later walking back to his hotel after covering a boxing show in Glasgow.

Another character on the Scottish desk liked to nip out for a taste whenever the job was running smoothly during often stormy evenings and early mornings. "Quick John" we called him. Once, denying he had taken the backstairs route to the adjacent pub rather than visit the "stone" where the pages were then prepared, he re-appeared without thinking his alibi through. He had forgotten to shake the incriminating snowflakes from his mop of black hair. A photographic veteran on the *Express* who had every chance of making progress with Manchester City as an inside forward until the war ended his personal "Blue Dream" in 1939 aged 18, would always take a single drink before he covered every game or any other photographic assignment. Aubrey Matthews would never wear anything but skyblue socks when he went behind the goals for a City game.

Every reporter in football has a "jobsworth" story. Sir Clem Freud was reporting for a quality Sunday newspaper deep in the South West. Clem discovered that he could catch the only convenient train to London by sharing the taxi ordered by the F.A. for the officials after the game. The referee was adamant and pompous. "Not possible," said the referee. "More than my job's worth." Sir Clem was thus relegated to the last train, arriving home early in the morning whereupon he rang the referee and roused him from a deep sleep. "Just thought you would be pleased to know I've just got back home," was all he said before putting the phone down.

My own "jobsworth" came when I needed urgently to talk to John Bond, then manager of Manchester City, at half time during a match at Oldham Athletic to discuss an important developing story. Bond was in the directors' lounge, a taboo area for journalists and anyone without the appropriate invitation. I knew Bond would step outside, if he got the message. "Can't help you – more than my job's worth," insisted the doorman in his gruffest manner. Then along strode Chief Superintendent Arthur Hardy, then in charge of the Oldham Division, who I had known since he was on the beat. "What's the problem, Derek?" he asked. Before I could explain my irritating little predicament the jobsworth had vanished, apparently deflated that his sense of authority had been usurped. John Bond was quite happy to emerge from the inner sanctum and answer my questions.

★

LANCASTER GATE, OFTEN condemned for being a few stars short of a galaxy long before the F.A. headquarters reached its peak of mischief and scandals in 2005, housed some bright administrator who had a brainwave before the Ipswich-Arsenal F.A. Cup Final in 1978. John Cobbold and his brother Patrick, both old Etonians *were* Ipswich and led the club with a social extravagance, expressing their disappointment and displeasure if guests left their boardroom other than replete. Legend has it that the brothers – John was marginally more extrovert than his brother - frequently embarked on tours of pubs in East Anglia owned by the family brewery, inevitably, of course, taking a drink at each hostelry. John, who needless to say could never be considered fit to drive, once decided to take the road to Newcastle for a match with his chauffeur. Both became so carried away on arrival at their hotel that they had to engage another sober driver to whisk them back to Suffolk.

To the Cobbolds, football was never less than fun. With the brothers liking for taking a drink in mind, an F.A. brightlight decided it would be appropriate to relieve them of undertaking travel arrangements for their mother, the formidably eccentric Lady Blanche, daughter of the Ninth Duke of Devonshire and with family links to Harold Macmillan, the former Tory Prime Minister, at Wembley for the greatest day in the history of Ipswich Town. Lady Blanche duly arrived in 'limo' splendour to join her sons in the VIP lounge at Wembley before the kick-off.

"Mother," asked John after ensuring that Lady Blanche was settled, "would you like to meet the Prime Minister (James Callaghan)?"

"No, thank you John," replied Lady Blanche, "I'd

much prefer a gin and tonic."

And Ipswich further brightened the day by beating Arsenal, Roger Osborne scoring the only goal in Ipswich's debut appearance in the Final. It is not recorded how long the Cobbold family celebrated their 100 per cent success rate in F.A. Cup finals! The aristrocatic Cobbolds hired the artisan Alf Ramsey and Bobby Robson to guide Ipswich through the glory years and released both without complaint or regard for insular preferences, to take over the campaign for England.

Len Shackleton had few friends at the Football Association, winning only five caps between 1949-55, a desperately unrewarding return for skills that entranced Sunderland supporters and thousands of neutrals across the nation. But Shack was Shack; outrageously talented, a Clown Prince of football, and always a rebel. That rebellious nature emerged in a chapter in his biography devoted to football club directors. It was a blank page. Shack worked for the *Daily Express*. He is said to be the first to have written that a team "started badly and fell away." He is also credited with observing that the "steel men" developed "metal fatigue" and may have been the first to pen that a tedious goalless draw was "much ado about nothing, nothing" which became a stand-by phrase, used when regarded as appropriate.

Those clichés came and went around the time some humorous journalist first penned that "defeat was snatched from the jaws of victory." Shackleton was also said to have half-volleyed a golf ball off the tee in frustration as his repeated failures to strike it accurately off a peg. He was also famous for deliberately imparting backspin to passes, the ball slowing in pace as teammates, including even the dashing centre forward Trevor Ford, struggled to take the ball in their stride.

Shack was an exciting player scoring six of the 13 goals without reply for Newcastle United against Newport in 1946 during the week he was transferred from Bradford Park Avenue. It may well have been Shackleton who first wrote the clever spoonerism "thud and blunder" inferring that the game been hard and clumsy in its style and not an epic red-blooded thriller.

★

JOURNALISTS, especially sports writers, are frequently told, "Your job must be the best in the world… watching sport across the globe and being paid for it." True, it is an enormous thrill but far more challenging (no, hair-raising at times) than the dear reader will ever know. *The Express* in Manchester received a well-written complaint from a Yorkshire reader; others were less literate and not free of invective. The bank employee challenged the quality of some of the reports he read in the edition circulating in Yorkshire, about half way through the night's production process. A polite "buzz off" letter stimulated rather than deterred the complainant. Finally the Sports Editor Mike Dempsey, vastly experienced and fair-minded, telephoned the 'wanna-be' and offered him the chance to be our reporter's guest at the next Sheffield Wednesday game and submit *his* report.

"No need to do a running report during the game, then top and tail it just before the final whistle like our reporter will be doing," wanna-be was told. "Also you can forget about the essential after-match checks and quotes. You can have half an hour to send us two to three hundred words.""How long?" queried the stunned wannabe, much in the same tone a Yorkshireman employs to demand 'how much?' when questioning the price of any commodity. "I thought I would have a few hours at least," wannabe wailed, evidently believing that some magical process delivered the edition to his doorstep at breakfast time. He never complained again.

Of course reporting sport, any sport, is a joy. There are, however, hazardous traps lurking behind every paragraph. It always seemed to be when the game has been a 0-0 bore, bereft of incident, only for the proceedings to erupt in a blaze of goals in the final 90 seconds. With the reasonable presumption that the game would end in goalless stalemate, a first edition story had to be hastily ad-libbed probably ten minutes from the end. Oops we've got goals... let's begin again. Small wonder grammatical (often in my case) and factual errors were inclined to creep in as the game, say, ended 2-1 or even worse, a cliffhanging 2-2.

Communications were always a problem until the advent of modern technology, even though reports can still vanish into the ether and computer systems crash. It is interesting to note here that it took hours until the advent of advanced technology for photographs to progress from the snapshot stage to the page, the time depending on the travelling disance to the subject and the availability of a 'wire' team. Camera to page now takes minutes.

One dour but desperately keen Rugby League

reporter was en route for Australia to cover a Test series for the *Daily Mirror* when his plane stopped for re-fuelling amid a major Middle East conflict. In the airport lounge, he snatched the chance to telephone to his office in Manchester a player injury up-date vital to the advance preview for the forthcoming Tests. Thrusting aside the gun pushed into his back by a dissident, he dutifully telephoned his copy to a background of the crackle (it is always a "crackle" in news dispatches) of small arms fire and the distant crunch of mortars. His bemused sports editor in Manchester ordered the copy to be shredded, desperately anxious for his Fleet Street office to remain unaware that his reporter had not informed them that he had the use of the one line out of the crisis zone while newsmen had been trying for hours to find a phone that worked and report urgently to the UK about a developing conflict.

The same zealous Rugby League reporter was involved in another cameo which summed up the rivalry and keenness in the sport. "Where's Joe?" a rival queried on the telephone one evening. "He's gone looking for peat," was the frank answer from the *Daily Mirror* sports desk. Rival Reporter hot-footed towards the Pennines, convinced that Joe had gone in search of Pete (his surname escapes me) who was the subject of a red hot story in Yorkshire Rugby League circles. Half way across the Pennines, he found keen gardener Joe... digging for peat.

★

In any language, gaining admission to the stadium is the

first hurdle. It proved insurmountable when I travelled with the trophy holders Manchester City to Katowice in the winter of 1971 to cover a Cup Winners' Cup quarter final. Unfortunately as I tried to gain entry to the press box a rifle butt barred my entrance to the main stadium and the tall tower high above the frostbound pitch. With Eastern Europe still in the grip of the enforced Communist regime, protests were not only ill-advised, but futile. It was a rare blip for the *Express* organisation for a reporter not to be in possession of the correct ticket; akin to being at immigration without a passport. I was escorted to the terraces, still with a smattering of snow from the winter.

Amazingly, my plight: no desk, no phone, no access to team titbits, no protection from the cold, immediately dawned on the Poles I sat among. They offered vodka and handshakes. My proffered hip flask of Scotch carried as a reserve for any emergency, was consumed by my new friends in toasts I did not understand. We had lift off. The squad had been in Spain to prepare for the start of their season after the winter break. That is why, I reasoned, the Polish players had tanned-looking legs. Surely they weren't wearing women's tights? The thought seemed absurd for such macho men but the Poles *were* wearing tights to warm their muscles in the freezing temperature, I was able to confirm from my bench close to the pitch.

My coverage was colourful and successful largely thanks to my new Polish friends. The Press box, I learned later, was stuffy, non-atmospheric and the view was desperately long range; disadvantages some scribes found difficult to overcome. City lost the game 2-0 but memorable but won the return by the same score and progressed after a play-off. Chelsea came next, City losing both legs 1-0. The tie against Chelsea saw Joe Mercer and his assistant Malcolm Allison in conflict. The suspended Allison urged that key players Mike Doyle and Colin Bell should be rested for a League game at Newcastle. Mercer insisted that they both played. Yes, you've guessed it. Both were injured and missed the vital game with Chelsea sweeping through to beat Real Madrid 2-1 in the replayed final in Athens after a 1-1 draw.

It should have been possible to forecast that my personal chaos in Katowice would be the sequel to the final between Manchester City and Gornik Zabrze. Vienna may be romantically beautiful and the Prater Stadium spick and span. Unfortunately it rained that night just after half time. No problem normally, except that the model stadium did not have a roof over any section of the stadium. Directors, players' wives – a pretty, well-dressed bunch they were, too - VIP's and of course the media pack, were drenched. Notes were washed away early in the second half. Water had to be poured out of the mouthpieces of telephones before reports of City's 2-1 success could be gurgled down the phone.

The media also got a soaking in Salonica for the final in the same competition three years later when AC Milan beat Leeds United 1-0. It never rained but it poured for sports journalist Bob Cass. While working for his national newspaper, Bob was asked to do a spot of stand-in radio reporting for a local station in the North East. The studio linkman was visiting each ground in turn seeking an up-date on the weather conditions as a prelim to the kick-offs. Bob, inexperienced then at broadcasting and not realising he was 'live' responded by proclaiming: "Its f.....g pissing down here, bonny lad."

My own broadcasting gaffe followed a cunning radio trap at the Queen's Park cricket ground while covering a rather slow-moving Derbyshire match. As my head went down in a comfortable doze, local prankster Mike Carey was on to it in a flash. He dived into the pavilion next to the press box and rang the phone under my nose. I was aroused with a start and answered a BBC production director in London who requested me to broadcast a 300 word report on the rather dour proceedings "in thirty seconds... counting from now, because there had been landline failures." As I had recently done some radio reporting for the BBC (North Region), I failed to smell a rat. However, I responded to the bogus cue-in lasting under half a minute with a not-too fluent ad-lib and put the phone down, heaving a sigh of relief. The Press Box applauded my efforts to a man. Only then did I discover that I had blurted my report to another telephone 30 feet away in the pavilion.

Pre-high-tech, some newspapers favoured using shorthand experts to note the reporter's dictated copy and then transfer it to a typewriter to begin the long and fraught process of publication. Ms X was expert at shorthand and was the choice of *The Guardian's* Alistair Cooke to handle his precious prose. Ms X also took dictated sports reports and was once distraught to discover when she began to transpose that she had used a similar outline for both boxers in a championship bout! On the *Express* we had one male copytaker who would seemingly struggle early in the afternoon to comprehend simple English or spell everyday names. In the evening after a swift half or two, the refreshed Tom would sail through your despatch... "Olarticoechea? Usual spelling?" he would chirp.

SOCCER ON THE INSIDE

IT HAS ALWAYS been a consistent sneer from management and players that soccer journos, and cricket writers know anything about the game because we never played it professionally. I do not recall that it is essential to be a musician to know if a fiddle is played in tune! In any case we all – reporters, spectators, avid fans - have played the game at some level or even at the highest - in our fantasies. I - a two-footed enthusiast with a bit of pace, had the unique privilege of playing behind one of the best wingers in the history of the game, and in front of a former captain of England and Great Britain - the marg between two slices of high fibre bread, as it were.

The occasion was a charity match at Oldham, with 20,000-plus in the ground to see the Showbiz stars and soccer greats like Sir Tom Finney, George Hardwick, Wally Barnes, Alex Forbes, Jack Rowley, Charlie Mitten, Jack Crompton, Freddy Pye, Sandy Busby and Mo Healey (who reported as Sir Harry of *Express Racing*) - he measured his football pace in yards rather than furlongs. The two former United stars, Rowley and Crompton, who after training practised saving the penalty kicks of Charlie Mitten, thus making them both experts, also gave their spare time to train the media mob. I was used as a brick wall with Sir Tom and Hardwick bouncing the ball off me as and when they chose.

My first pass to Tom was a probing Lancashire Amateur League (Southern Section) type of pass down the right flank vaguely in the direction of Chadderton for Tom to chase. Sir Tom stopped, turned sharply and with a hint of admonishment and presumably sympathy for my inadequacies, jabbed a finger at himself, clearly indicating that he expected the ball to be directed to his person, not into the wilderness of Boundary Park. All the old pros were in retirement, but their skills and technique were undiminished, if deployed at a more sedate pace. The privilege of playing in such accomplished company served as a reminder of the cavernous cavity in ability between the enthusiastic amateur and the seasoned pro in any sport. Watching was enough to outline the gap; being involved at close quarters even at the pace of friendlies added heavy emphasis. It is worth noting here the simple statistics of Sir Tom's unblemished time on the soccer stage: 433 League games, 107 goals, 76 England caps, ONE CLUB.

Mind you, some scribes took unusual short cuts into the pro ranks. Gary Talbot was an experienced national newspaper photographer and keen local league footballer. After watching Chester waste innumerable chances in one match, Gary told the then manager, Peter Hauser: "I can play a bit - no worse than your lot.". "Oh yes, I've heard that one before... show me then," said Hauser. Talbot did - and served the club with distinction and a flow of goals. Another former journalist Bob Kelly made headlines of his own when he took over as manager of Leicester City. Kelly completed his formal training on a Wolverhampton evening paper where his ambition was to become a news reporter rather than specialise in sport, before launching a career in coaching. He took over from Craig Levein.

Paul Hince, of the *Manchester Evening News*, was a zippy but hardly gutsy winger for Manchester City, Charlton and Crewe where he was a team-mate of Peter Leigh, captain of the club and a former "Blue" himself. Peter was the perfect pro – a football beacon at any level of the game. He was proud to have encouraged his team-mate Stan Bowles, a colourful and skilful player who never fully developed his skills as a player, to cut back on his gambling. The gutsy Leigh and the less than dedicated Bowles were perfect examples of talent maximised and talent wasted.

Gerry Harrison joined *The Express* from Oxford (University not United) and played at left back during Altrincham's adventures that made them the non-League giants of the F.A. Cup, before switching media and making his career as a TV soccer reporter. Few footballers could become journalists without the aid of ghost writers though there were notable exceptions in the likes of Danny Blanchflower, Len Shackleton and Ivor Broadis who joined the ranks of full time journalists. Genuine journalists including David Harrison (Panorama) the brother of Gerry, David Miller (*Telegraph*) Tony Pawson (*Observer*), Geoffrey Green (*Times*) and David Icke (TV) all played football to a high level with university or respected amateur clubs before becoming full time scribes. Donny Davies was by-lined "Old International" by *The Guardian* for obvious reasons and Green was once described by the legendary Charles Buchan as "the best centre half in England, amateur or professional," before a leg injury ended his football fun..

THE SUMMER GAME

CRICKET LOVELY CRICKET

JIM LAKER ENJOYED relating the story about being picked to play for the Combined Services before his demob. Then, all-rounder Jim was a batsman/bowler rather than the specialist off-spinner who ravaged the Aussies, taking 19 wickets on a spinners' paradise at Old Trafford in 1956. Laker was number eight in the Combined Services batting order with "an unknown to me, Jack Fallows, named as one of the openers." Laker made inquiries and found that Fallows as a Lieutenant Colonel "pulled rank" on Cpl. Laker in compiling the batting order. "That explained everything," Laker, who wrote a column for the *Daily Express*, said later. Fallows was a popular stand-in captain of Lancashire for one season in 1946 and later became a respected and humorous committee member.

Laker was modesty personified. Who else could have strolled so nonchalantly to the pavilion at Old Trafford with his sweater slung over his shoulders after taking all but one of the twenty Aussie wickets to fall in July 1956. Laker took 9-37 in the first innings and followed that with figures of 10-53, the only time a Test bowler had been so outrageously successful. The previous best bowling performance in England-Australia clashes was 8-35 by one G. Lohmann of Surrey in 1886-87. Laker seemed to be saying "That wasn't such a bad performance after all." The histrionics were later to become so ostentatious that even a delivery of perfect length and line often merited a BAFTA-rated performance, presumably for the benefit of the ever-increasing scrutiny of the television cameras

Cricket, it always seemed, was played with a smile during the day followed by a beer in the pavilion. That bonhomie may well have arisen from the absence of serious financial implications, although the rivalry was never less than serious. No rivalries were more intense on the field and more convivial off it than between two legendary cavaliers of cricket Denis Compton and Keith Miller, the Aussie who flew nightfighters during the war, disappointingly not as a wing commander or even a squadron leader, but as a non-commissioned flight sergeant. Miller was magnificent with bat or ball, his black hair flying in every direction, though he secretly combed it after every varied over. Compton was a schoolboy dream of a player, once, I can vividly recall, losing his balance as he darted down the wicket to play a forcing forward shot, only to recover by late-cutting the delivery for four.

It was almost a relief to learn years later that Compton had a weakness – his running between the wickets was, at the least, unpredictable. "When Denis called 'come one' it was regarded as a basis for negotiation," recalled one veteran. Once stumps were drawn, Compton and Miller were first into the bar and first to leave together for a night on the town, though there was never any photographic evidence to support the delightful story that either one of them, or may be both, appeared in the dressing next morning still attired in a dinner jacket.

Cricketers, in my sports reporting days at least, always seemed to have a sharper sense of humour and were more likely to produce the colourful phrase. No-one knows which bowler first declared after seeing an opening batsman play and widely miss his first three snorting deliveries: "I'll bowl you a piano next – see it you can play that!" Nor is it recorded which batsman confided to a bowler: "You had me in two minds in that over – I didn't know whether to hit you for six or four."

Clive Lloyd, the gangling, amiable captain of Lancashire and the West Indies, featured in many successful partnerships with Harry Pilling, at least a foot shorter, during the Red Rose county's dominant era in one-day cricket. Pilling once observed that batting with Clive "was like batting with a f.....g big black spider." A colourful observation. Lloyd was once asked by Mike Denness in the crucial last over before lunch against Kent: "How many left Clive?" "One, Mike," replied one captain to the other. Denness turned to the umpire and inquired: "How many left umpire?" "One skipper," replied the puzzled official. "Perhaps you're happy now you've got it in black *and* white," Lloyd mumbled as he ambled towards deep mid-off.

It always amuses me to relate a true story concerning Graeme Atkinson who had come up from Somerset to open Lancashire's batting and subsequently became a Rugby League official. Most Sunday mornings I would meet Graeme, his wife and daughters, about the same age as my two, in a local swimming baths. It surprised, if not shocked, the assembled gathering when I once mischievously announced to Mrs. Atkinson at a social function at Old Trafford: "Sorry, luv, I didn't recognise you with your clothes on!" Such verbal slapstsick was, unfortunately, rare to surface in my reporting duties.

A close friend must have had a strong sense of humour not to have ended the friendship there and then at Headingley. He had whisked the lass off to watch a Roses match a matter of hours after they ended up in Yorkshire for a holiday with friends. Days later they were at Headingley again to watch Fred Trueman make his Test debut. The lass had perused the scorecards and observed the asterisk denoting captain on the scorecard for both club and country matches and was finally moved to inquire: "Just how many captains does this club have?" Oddly, they stayed together and lived happily ever after.

KERRY PACKER

IT MAY HAVE taken football some time to recover from the lifting of the maximum wage bondage in 1961 and the Bosman ruling barring transfer fees for players out of contract 35 years later, but cricket was hit for six when Kerry Packer dangled massive financial carrots and induced the world's top 35 Test players to up stumps and join his World Series Cricket circus under floodlights playing in coloured kit and with a white ball. Lord's was apoplectic, crying "no ball." Establishment figures snubbed the 'rebel' players, some of whom incurred the wrath of their bretheren in white flannels for their defection. But Packer, as Jean Marc Bosman had also been obliged to do, took his case to court and won. Packer brought a High Court case against cricket's establishment which lasted three weeks and cost the wealthy Aussie media mogul, who owned Australia's Channel Nine TV station, a fortune he could well afford. It was a resounding victory over restraint of trade.

WSC was barred from all major cricket grounds and was obliged to transport pitches into unfamiliar venues such as the Sydney Showground and Melbourne's VFL Park. Packer's coup revolutionised cricket with the help of the game's best players including England captain Tony Greig and Aussie skipper Greg Chappell. What could in certain stalemate circumstances be a three or five day drudge to those without a feeling for and knowledge of the real magic of the game, were lured by Packer's crusade to bring the game to the masses who became entranced by the instant action of limited overs cricket. Where the BBC had used four cameras to cover a game, Packer introduced eight with the batsman on strike always facing the probing lens. Sound effects microphones brought the game into homes via the airwaves.

Bob Parish, chairman of the Australian Cricket Board was later obliged to admit: "Kerry Packer and World Series did the game a favour. If we had tried as a board in 1979 to play limited-overs cricket with coloured clothing using white balls, our chances of getting it to happen would have been virtually nil." The players who joined the circus were shunned by the MCC and after agonising over the decisions began to count the cost

– in pound notes. Pre-Packer pay cheques were modest. County players of the highest calibre were paid less than £3000 a year, often earning more in the winter from part-time employment than they did in the summer.

Test match fees in 1977 were £200 for a five-day game watched by large crowds on the grounds and by millions in homes on TV. That modest Test fee had increased by only £20 in a decade. There was talk of players being offered between £10-15,000 for three-year deals for only two months work. That said, the players earned their money. Bob Woolmer, the former Kent and England batsman who later coached Pakistan, was to recall: "As players we did not know what to expect when we went to Australia and nor did the public, who in the first year were unsure whether everyone would be taking the experiment seriously. They soon found out and so did I. Walking out to bat with Dennis Amiss in one match played 'up country', I recall the fast bowler Lenny Pascoe snarling that he would put us both in hospital by the end of the day. Given the condition of the wicket, it was no idle threat.

"We were often playing on some very uneven surfaces in what was the first widespread use of drop-in pitches where turf was specially provided for matches. In fact, it was a time of real innovation not just with the coloured clothing and floodlights which became so popular. Helmets became the norm and it was the first time that extra padding was used on the inside thigh, for example. (It brings tears to the eyes to recall that in the lusty Bodyline series in Australia, players used gloves, pads, a box, a cap or green "baggie" as protection). The crowds really got into it in the second year and were bigger than for the official Tests that went on at the same time in Australia."

Packer, whose revolution led to the game later becoming so vibrant in its new form, died at Christmas 2005 aged 68, two months after Robert, later Lord, Alexander, 69, whose elegance in the High Court helped the ruthless Aussie to win his case. Packer's revolution did not rest happily with those who believed in the traditional format. Brian Close, captain courageous of Yorkshire, was adamantly opposed to the revolution and talked about cricket 'clown' gear. His stance played no small part in his fall-out with the White Rose.

Bob Paisley had a love of cricket back dating back to his roots in his native County Durham. He became a popular guest of captain Jack Bond, in the Lancashire dressing room, and was once asked during a game at Aigburth if he could volunteer his services as a physiotherapist. "No problem," said the amiable Bob, whose other sporting interest was horseracing, occasionally riding out for his trainer pal Frank Carr. The injured cricketer had a trace of hypochondria, so knowing this Bob diagnosed the treatment of dipping the injured elbow into a bowl of water "charged" by a lifeless strip of electric cable. The treatment was wholly successful.

Most sports hacks, when cricket always seemed to be played in the "lazy, hazy days of summer" had a sense of honour. Not every story would be reported in soccer either to spare players or clubs acute embarrassment. Such "selectivity" would result in a P64 for reporters in subsequent years. Though well behind the soccer stars, our cricketers moved up the cash ladder in winning the Ashes in 2005 to be given football status as a TV spectacular with massive popular appeal. The bat and ball men were obliged to earn their wages – sometimes there was a suspicion that footballers didn't always do so – and the schedule the ECB agreed to after the winter's graft in Pakistan and India looked designed to guarantee cricket fatigue and travel sickness.

Previous Press tourists to India and Pakistan, incidentally, had a rota of additional responsibilities to ensure the comfort of the tourists. It was considered essential on tour that there was always a supply of Mars bars to hand for those with digestive systems unable to cope, with curry and whisky for those who thought they could. The 2006-7 Ashes venture Down Under was insensitively sandwiched into 45 days, the whole programme including Champions Trophy and World Cup matches stretching over three months from November to February, 2007. All of which followed a summer series in England. Even the scribes and TV pundits required the stamina of marathon runners and anti-mental block pills to keep up with such a whirlwind pace.

A cricket lesson was learned when I captained a newspaper team in a Sunday match at York against the Nondescripts. My sports editor had arranged for "Collie" (O'Neil Gordon) Smith, the West Indian who was viewed by many as a challenger to Sir Gary Sobers as the outstanding all-rounder in world class cricket, to boost our side. Though an outfielder with a reasonable reliable pair of hands, I fielded at second slip alongside Collie, who I had not met before, to make social contact.

Early in the Nondescripts innings, a left-hander flashed wildly at a decent delivery from Ted Hart. Collie, inspired by the success of Jim Laker to switch from pace to off-spin, caught the ball one handed by his left ankle and was tossing it back to Ted before I or the wicket-keeper Wilf Dowding, who put journalism before the chance of a possible career in cricket, had moved.

Tragically, Collie, who had played for Burnley in the Lancashire League for two summers, was aged only 26 and some way off his peak as a player, when he was killed in a car crash near Stoke-on-Trent shortly after that game at York. Sir Gary escaping serious injury. Garfield Sobers, then a 23-year-old Barbadian all-rounder, was the world's best player, having rattled up 365 in Trinidad six months previously. Smith, known around the globe as 'Collie', was rated number two and both were first capped against the Aussies in 1954-55. In his biography of Sobers (Collins, 1976) Trevor Bailey wrote: "They were mates and very close. They roomed together, liked the same things, laughed at the same jokes and both had an all-absorbing love for cricket. There was never any jealousy, just tremendous mutual admiration and understandings."

Gary and Collie had picked up Tom Dewdney, 25, a tall fast bowler with nine Test caps, in Manchester for a night drive to London when they crashed in Staffaordshire. Two days later Collie, an orphan raised in the heart of Kingston's poorest district at Boys' Town, died. More than 100,000 people attended Smith's funeral in Boys' Town. Smith's death was a turning point in the life of Sobers. He wrote in his 1988 autobiography:

"With Collie (he drank pints of orange juice after our game in York) gone, I began to drink heavily. Collie had been the stabilising influence in my life. Not that he was puritanical, he loved enjoying himself as much as I did, but if I had shown signs of going too far he would always say 'steady, that's enough for tonight. Let's go home.'" It is appropriate here to record that several team-mates at Manchester United had tried in vain to urge the same restraints on Best.

Trevor Bailey wrote: "Gary was determined now to crowd into his own life as much pleasure as possible for, after all, it was only fate that he should live and Collie should die." Sobers was still grieving when Peter May's England arrived in the West Indies. Sir Gary announced he would be "batting for Collie." In the first Test at Barbados, he made 226 (b. Fred Trueman) out of 563. Before the Jamaica Test at Collie's home ground, Sabina Park, Frank Keating of *The Guardian* was to recall, he met Smith's Boys' Town mentor and guardian Father Hugh Sherlock. He, apparently, inspired Collie's ambition to follow the life pattern of England's batsman David Shepard who became Bishop of Liverpool, but who was irreverently rebuked by Fred Trueman after a dropped catch in the slips: "The only time tha gets thee hands together is when tha's praying." Those who had the pleasure of his jovial company as team-mate and opponent have one special member with a special cricket memory – the bowler who dismissed Collie Smith for the last time for thirtysomething. A few weeks earlier Smith had hammered 306 for Burnley against Lowerhouse, a league record in one-day cricket.

ODDS AND SODS

CUP COUPS

ANY CUP ROMANTIC could not fail to have been impressed by my home town club. Altrincham had a record 16 successes against Football League teams in reaching the F.A. Cup fourth round proper and the third round seven times between 1966 and 1995. The Robins hit the first round a total of 11 times between 1922 and 1997 as soccer cavaliers who regularly used to win over the hearts of the neutral masses. A 2-1 victory over Birmingham City at St. Andrew's in 1985-6 was rated a major triumph.

Two years earlier Manchester United, whose shadow spreads out the eight miles to Altrincham and beyond, proved their fallibility by allowing Bournemouth to oust them 2-0. Nothing quickens the pulse more than a cracking cup tie whether on the terraces or in the press box. A touch of farce can help, too. It took political upheaval to shift opinion at Lancaster Gate. Many pairs of sleepy eyes were opened by a break with tradition for season 1999-2000 that must have shaken the foundations of the Association's headquarters. First, the F.A. abandoned the traditional timing of the third round switching it from its January date to before Christmas. Gates slumped so it was back to square one the following season, but not before a touch of the bizarre. Incredibly

United were allowed to skip the 1999-2000 campaign to take part in FIFA's first World Cup Championship in Brazil early in the New Year. It got worse. To make up for the odd number of clubs in the hat for the Third Round, some whiz kid decided on a farcical "lucky losers" draw among the clubs that exited in Round Two. Darlington, beaten at Gillingham, went into the front line again and lost 2-1 at Aston Villa. Knocked out twice in the same fight takes some beating.

Almost every freak occurrence it seems has happened in the F.A. Cup. The odds must have huge against 16 different players scoring all the goals in the semi-final ties of 1990 won 4-3 by Crystal Palace in beating Liverpool and in the 3-3 and 2-1 encounters between Manchester United and Oldham Athletic. Comebacks, calamities, catastrophies and comedy spice the Cup, the underdogs enjoying a spell of having their day every 17 years. In 1955, York City of the old Third Division North stretched Newcastle to a semi-final replay after beating Tottenham among others in a record sprint for a Third Division side. Then in 1972, non-league Hereford United beat First Division Newcastle in a mud bath at Edgar Street after a replay. On to 1989 when non-League Sutton United toppled First Division Coventry leaving Burton, Northwich and Nuneaton Borough, and Tamworth from the Nationwide Conference to attempt to maintain the 17-year itch.

★

LEN SHACKLETON, the rogue Sunderland star admitted, after a remarkable comeback from 3-0 down, "we were so bad in the first half we were lucky to get nil." One manager complained that all six goals whipped past his defence had been breakaways. Bobby Gould was more drastic during Peterborough United's 1-0 defeat at Bristol City in the LDV Vans Trophy first round tie in 2004 – he quit, at half-time, as head coach.

Though there was not a happy ending, the campaign of Chasetown in 2005 even viewed from long range had an engaging appeal. Chasetown? Few had heard of a village with a population of around 5,000 on the outskirts of Walsall until they were drawn against Oldham Athletic in the first round of the tournament before failing in a replay to bring off (statistically) the biggest shock in the history of the game's oldest competition.

The traditional collection of a postman, a road digger, carpet fitters, lorry drivers, labourers and a fitness centre manager graced the Harvey World Travel Midland Alliance Stadium, no less than seven divisions and 130 places below their visitors at the real kick-off of the 2005-6 campaign. They earned their £20 (plus £10 for a win) in front of crowds of just over 100 with the biggest gate reaching 144 until they drew in around 2,000 for a historic fourth qualifying round success over Blyth Spartans, a team of renowned cup warriors from the North East. This time the "Scholars" lunchtime tie was screened live on BBC TV's Match of the Day watched by millions around the world with a windfall of around £80,000.

Alarm bells must have rung as Manchester United, so soon after their disastrous flop in Portugal against their old rivals Benfica, set out for a third round tie against

Burton Albion of the Conference managed, as they had to be in the circumstances, by Nigel Clough, son of Brian, born a few months before England's triumph in the 1966 World Cup. You could imagine the words of advice from father to son: "Go for it, son. Show them you can play football. They will be worried sick about your lads." Sons of famous fathers like Liam Botham or the Nicklaus sons in golf do not have an easy time. Nigel, a player with Nottingham Forest, Liverpool and Manchester City as well as 14 times for England – seven times more than his dad – could not escape comparisons as a player. But with a club of Burton's modest background, he was free of correlations with his father who served his apprenticeship in management at a higher level.

"I'm certain he won't follow me into football management," Clough Snr wrote in his autobiography published in 1994. With respect to the family's quirky nature, Brian should have known better than to make that prediction, though he believed living near the Pirelli Stadium built on the back of Nigel's success and popularity "was being too comfortable – life's not like that." Nigel must have had confusing thoughts before he declined to switch the biggest game in a 55-year-old history, from the snug Burton stadium to the wider expanses of Derby County where his father weaved his managerial magic. A richly deserved draw was as near as Albion came to achieving arguably the biggest shock in the history of the competition. Defeat at Old Trafford in the replay saw around 11,000 fans travel from Burton, happy in retrospect to visit the 'Theatre of Dreams' where they hoped to see a cup tragedy for followers of United.

A boost to the bank balance of approaching a million pounds did much to ease the pain of a 5-0 defeat.

Yeovil have a special niche in the history of the F.A. Cup in becoming the top giant killers with victories over Colchester United and Blackpool in 2000-01. Those successes rolled up into a total of 20 F.A. Cup wins against League opposition. Yeovil, formerly of the infamous tilting pitch, also set another non-League milestone by becoming victors in the Third Round 13 times. It is safe to assume that a non-league team will never win the Cup Final again or even reach the Final. Yet three times since the League was formed in 1888 three non-Leaguers have made it to the final. Sheffield Wednesday (Football Alliance) were second best in 1890 hammered 6-1 by Blackburn Rovers. Southampton (Southeren League) made it in 1900, losing 4-0 to Bury and were at the summit again two years later, beaten 2-1 by Sheffield United after extra time. Spurs as a Southern League outfit went one better, beating Sheffield United 3-1 at Burnden Park, then the home of Bolton Wanderers, after a 2-2 draw.

Up to 2005, five non-league clubs had battled through to the fifth round... Colchester United (1948), Yeovil (1949), Blyth Spartans (1978), Telford (1984) and Kidderminster (1994). It was a bleak year for the "minnows" in 1951 when not a single non-league outfit reached Round Three.

It was a personal boast and a particular joy that I played in two F.A. Cup ties, though I was never quick to add that I was on the wrong end of 6-1 scorelines on both occasions and that the ties were in the Cheshire

Senior Cup, not the Football Association Challenge Cup! I can recall meriting only one press mention for my campaigning in the F.A. Cup or anywhere else for that matter: "Potter, on leave from the RAF, had a good game at outside left and was unlucky not to score." The greater joy came from never consciously being involved in any unsightly spats that can haunt the game during my career; a few personal skirmishes, yes, but none that lasted beyond the moment.

WEMBLEY ONE-OFFS

WEMBLEY CUP FINALS have oozed stories of desperation, joy, good luck, desperate misfortune, comedy and tragedy since the first at the stadium in 1923 when a single policeman on a white horse restored law and order as thousands of the crowd, many of whom had gained admission without a ticket, flooded on to the pitch. One story underlines the popularity of the event, especially when the big clubs are involved, and the clamour for tickets. Two friends, one a freelance journalist and the other with an entrepreneurial streak, were approaching Wembley for the 1990 Final between Manchester United and Crystal Palace. "Quick son, give me your ticket," was the surprising demand from "Mr. Fixit."

Five minutes later he was back and thrust £300 into the hands of the surprised and disappointed journalist who supported Palace and was desperate to watch his first Final. "The black market's red hot – too good a chance to miss," he explained. "We'll drive north towards home and nip into a pub to watch the Final." They found their pub, but 15 minutes from the kick-off, the publican ordered them out of the TV Room. "Sorry, regulars only," he explained. "Mr. Fixit," with a performance worthy of a RADA scholarship, related a tear-jerking "we wuz robbed" story. "That's real bad luck, lads," said the sympathetic landlord, "come in take a seat for the match - and have a drink on the house." Final over – it was a 3-3 draw – the landlord pulled the Northern pair to one side. "Here you are lads," he said. "It's not been your day. We had a whip round for you in the TV room." He thrust £40 into "Mr. Fixit's" extended hand. And so many of us north of Birmingham believed that southerners were a tight-fisted lot.

The Palace freelance fan later went (unaccompanied by "Mr. Fixit") to the replay without any pre-match deviations, only to see his heroes lose 1-0. "Mr. Fixit," oblivious to the questionable morality of his private enterprise, enjoyed telling the story of his black market enterprise. And yes, he did retire happily and well off in the Italian Lakes. A personal "old" Wembley howler was my concern that there was seemingly only one whisky 'White Horse' available in the stadium media area. How stupid to forget that the first Final at Wembley in 1923 when Bolton Wanderers beat West Ham United 2-0, was everlastingly famous for the solitary PC riding a white horse who restored order after thousands left the dangerously overcrowded terraces to invade the pitch.

★

'OLD' WEMBLEY must have seemed like home to the eight players who appeared in five Finals, replays excluded.

★ Joe Hume – Arsenal: 1927, lost; 1930 won; 1932 lost; 1936 won; Huddersfield Town: 1938 lost.

★ Johnny Giles – Manchester United: 1963 won; Leeds United: 1965 lost; 1970 drew, lost replay, 1972 won; 1973 lost.

★ Pat Rice – Arsenal: 1971 won; 1972 lost; 1978 lost; 1979 won; 1980 lost.

★ Frank Stapleton – Arsenal: 1978 lost; 1979 won; 1980 lost; Manchester United: 1983 won; 1985 won

★ Ray Clemence – Liverpool: 1971 lost; 1974 won; 1977 lost; Tottenham: 1982 won; 1987 lost.

★ Mark Hughes – Manchester United: 1985 won; 1990 won; 1994 won; 1995 lost; Chelsea: 1997 won.

★ John Barnes – Watford: 1984 lost; Liverpool: 1988 lost; 1989 won; 1996 lost; Newcastle United: 1998, sub, lost. Barnes became the first player to lose Wembley finals with three different clubs.

★ Roy Keane – Nottingham Forest: 1991 lost; Manchester United: 1994 won; 1995 lost; 1996 won; 1999 won.

★ FINALNOTE 1: Stapleton, Clemence and Hughes also played in replays making six Wembley appearances each.

★ FINALNOTE 2: Glenn Hoddle also made six Cup Final appearances: 5 for Tottenham, including 2 replays in 1981, 1982, and 1987 and one for Chelsea as sub in 1994.

★ SICKNOTE: Paul Bracewell played in four Finals without being a winner. Everton: 1985, 1986, 1989; Sunderland: 1992.

Sir Alex Ferguson topped the winning manager's

league in 2004 with his fifth appearance following Finals in 1990, 1994, 1996, 1999. Sir Alex had no excuses for Wembley nerves, but Alan Davies of Manchester United did in 1983 when he made his Cup debut in the Final against Brighton. Also excused Cup jitters were debutants Chris Baird (Southampton v Arsenal in 2003) and Curtis Weston as a sub for Millwall against Manchester United in 2004. Dennis Wise (Millwall, 2004) became the third player with the twin role as player-manager, following Kenny Dalglish (Liverpool, 1986) and Glenn Hoddle (Chelsea 1994).

'Old' Wembley with its famous Twin Towers had an inspirational charm – or a terror for the timid players – all of its own. When Wembley was re-built at cost three times larger than Cardiff's Millennium Stadium where the F.A. happily took refuge. With 90,000 seats the new Wembley will rival stadia/stadiums (experts still argue over the plural) like the Nou Camp, Bernabeu and the Azteca where the first view takes the breath away.

For the over-exciteable or emotionally challenged, the number of toilets was increased to 2,618 compared with 361 at the old stadium. The famous skip or trudge (win or lose) up to the Royal Box (every one of the seats has more legroom that royalty enjoyed in the old RB), to collect the Cup was increased from a mere 39 steps to 107. Wembley seemed ever farther away to player and fan than it did.

EPILOGUE

A CLOSE ASSOCIATION with the Merseyside clubs began early in my career with the *Express*. Liverpool were promoted from the old Second Division in 1962 heading Leyton Orient by eight points and Sunderland by nine to end seven seasons of failure compared with the subsequent years of roaring success. Happily for me and the *Express*, Everton won the First Division title in the freeze-up the following season and Liverpool began their magnificent march to glory by claiming the title the following season, four points clear of Manchester United and five ahead of the holders Everton.

Liverpool then broke their 73-year F.A. Cup duck with Ian St. John gliding in towards the near post to head a cross by Ian Callaghan and end the extra time battle with Leeds United. "We were all tired, so I reasoned that Ian would not have the energy to hit the ball as full as usual, so I moved in towards him," the shrewd St. John said afterwards. After the championship success of 1964 four points ahead of Manchester United and six in front of Everton, Liverpool accepted an invitation to tour the U.S.A. winding up in Vancouver for five professionally successful and eminently social weeks as soccer ambassadors. I was one of two national newspaper reporters to make the tour, winding up in Vancouver where we had a couple of days rest.

During the wind-down to an exhausting schedule, I pondered the joy at reporting games and enjoying social and humorous events; by later standards of professional conduct, I would have been rapped, at least, for not reporting some of the incidents in New York, Chicago, Boston, St. Louis, San Francisco, and finally British Columbia, flying home through Toronto. Friendships with players, directors and management, particularly Bob Paisley and Reuben Bennett, developed during the tour were later to be of enormous value to me and the *Daily Express*.

It was an unexpected career bonus for the former office boy at the *Altrincham Guardian*. I decided, on impulse, to send a postcard to my first boss, Mr. Beattie, who gave me my start, explaining apologetically that the best wage he could offer to a 16-year-old was thirty bob (150p) a week for my exclusive services. Our relationship became more informal and personal as my career advanced, aged 24, to National newspaper level much to Mr. Beattie's pleasure. "Mr. Beattie," duly became "Arthur" and we met socially.

"Dear Arthur," I wrote from Vancouver on a Devonshire Hotel postcard, "I'm just finishing a memorable tour of the US and Canada with Liverpool FC meeting some fine people and visiting some fabulous places. If it wasn't for you, I wouldn't be here! Thanks for the start you gave me."

The day after receiving the card at his home in Altrincham, some 5,000 miles from Vancouver, Arthur died. It was the most important few words among countless thousands I wrote.

DEREK POTTER

Former Daily Express sports writer

The death of Derek Potter last month, at the age of 75, was the breaking of another link with the days, in the '60s and '70s, when English football seemed to be alive with legends.

One of them, the great Manchester United and Scotland striker Denis Law, attended the funeral in Cheshire, together with many of the journalist's friends and colleagues.

Potter was a quiet, warm man, in a business that could be ruthless, but he acquired a reputation as a great newsgatherer — one that was augmented by the award of sports reporter of the year for his revelation that Robert Maxwell was attempting to buy Manchester United — a story of the '80s that anticipated the corporate future of England's major football clubs.

In a stream of tributes from football and journalism, there was one constant theme — Potter was a man who could be trusted.

He spent his entire career in his native northwest of England, the perfect place for a football reporter determined to operate at the heart of the national game.

He travelled widely across Europe with all the leading clubs and was close to all the great managers

— and their players.

Gordon Taylor, chief executive of the Professional Fooballers' Association, attended the funeral and said: "Whenever you were interviewed by Derek, you knew whatever you said would be faithfully reported. He didn't spin the news, he reported it, operating on the basis that there is never anything so sensational as the truth."

Potter started his career on local papers in Cheshire, but quickly graduated to the *Daily Mirror* in Manchester, from where he was soon signed by that paper's greatest rival in those days, *The Express*.

His enduring ability to land the big story led to his one mis-step in a superbly professional career. Soon after he won his sports reporter of the year award, and long after becoming a senior and much respected figure in *The Express's* famous glass-fronted office in Ancoats Street, Manchester, he was tempted to join the new *Today* newspaper.

At the time, he said he welcomed a new challenge, but unfortunately he fell victim to redundancy measures when the newspaper slipped towards extinction. The manner of his parting spoke of harsher days in the newspaper business. Such a career development would have embittered a man of less grace; instead, he shrugged his shoulders and worked as a freelance.

Former *Express* writer Derek Hodgson spoke of the dilemma faced by Potter's family and colleagues, debating whether or not something representative of a great reporter's life should be placed in the coffin.

One suggestion was that it should be his mobile phone, but Vera Potter demurred. "I don't see the point," she said, "Derek always had it switched off."

James Lawton
Reproduced from www.pressgazette.co.uk

INDEX

INDEX

INDEX

The Story of the
GREEN & GOLD
Newton Heath 1878-1902
CHARBEL BOUJAOUDE
FOREWORD BY IAIN MCCARTNEY
£10.95 - PAPERBACK - 312 PP

THE GREEN AND GOLD campaign launched recently by Manchester United fans against the club's owners, the Glazer family, took its inspiration from the colours of the original Newton Heath club from which United emerged in 1902. This book attempts to explain the characters and history of that club.

Relying on extensive research, the author brings to life a late Victorian era where football mushroomed to become the national pastime. The cast of characters who formed the club are profiled in detail – Sam Black, the Doughty brothers, Jack Peden and John Cassidy were legends on the pitch while Mr Albut, the chairman, was charged with the often impossible task of making ends meet by whatever means neccessary of it.

The supporters, many of whom now had more leisure time thanks to that brand new Mancunian invention, the 'weekend', turned up in increasing numbers at the club's first ground at North Road, Monsall, which became infamous for the depth of its mud and later followed the team to Bank Street, Clayton where nearby factories would judiciously belch out a chemical smog whenever Heath needed 'assistance'.

Unfortunately, Heath's financial health took a turn for the worse following a ruinous court case. The debts dragged the club slowly but surely toward bankruptcy and a date with destiny. By 1902 a decade of Second Division anonymity, ever-decreasing quality on the field and mounting debts forced the club to the brink and, eventually, via Harry Stafford's famous dog, the salvation of local brewing magnate John Henry Davies and the formation of Manchester United.

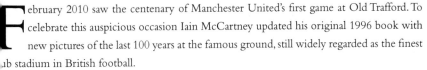
February 2010 saw the centenary of Manchester United's first game at Old Trafford. To celebrate this auspicious occasion Iain McCartney updated his original 1996 book with new pictures of the last 100 years at the famous ground, still widely regarded as the finest club stadium in British football.

Constructed in 1909 and officially opened on 19th February 1910 for the league visit of Liverpool, Old Trafford was instantly acclaimed by one reporter as "the most handsomest [sic], the most spacious and the most remarkable arena I have ever seen. As a football ground it is unrivalled in the world, it is an honour to Manchester and the home of a team who can do wonders when they are so disposed."

Unfortunately the stadium arrived at just the wrong time for the club as after winning the championship again in 1911 United were about to embark on a 37 year trophy-free run, the longest in the club's history. Consequently, United's average attendance before the war rarely topped the 30,000 mark, in a ground with a capacity of over 70,000. The luckless stadium suffered further blows on the nights of the 8th and 11th March 1941 when it was bombed during The Manchester Blitz and so for four seasons after the war United were forced to play 'home' fixtures at Maine Road.

The arrival of floodlights and European football heralded a new chapter: the stadium is widely regarded as at its best on such occasions and from the first game against the immortals of Real Madrid in 1957 the ground hosted continental opposition and became renowned across Europe.

However these improvements were as nothing compared to the dramatic changes brought about in the wake of the Taylor Report. The birth of the Premier League and United's domestic dominance helped transform the ground

Calling on the vast photographic resources of avid Manchester United collectors and enthusiasts, what emerges is a fascinating history of the first super stadium of English football. It also traces the history of United via its home ground, from the post WWI football boom, to the bomb damage sustained during the Manchester Blitz and the 8 year wait for the stadium to be fully re-built and the beginning, in the mid 1960s, of terrace hooliganism and the club's attempts to deal with it. Now the stadium, a vast arena holding over 75,000 seats, is valued at over £230m. Not bad for a patch of land once given over to cattle grazing.

THE COMPLETE
ERIC CANTONA

EVERY GAME - EVERY GOAL
by Darren Phillips

ISBN: 1901746585 - 9781901746587

£10.95 - PAPERBACK - 308 PP

ERIC CANTONA'S CAREER at Old Trafford lasted only 5 years but its lasting impa[ct] can still be felt today. During that comparatively small span, Cantona's dedication an[d] self-confidence enabled a club to emerge from over a quarter of a century of failu[re] and self-doubt.

Cantona's career before he arrived in England had been nomadic at best, self-destructive [at] worst. He blazed a trail through French football but the highest profile incidents centred on h[is] spectacular misbehaviour and clashes with authority. By the time he was snapped up by Lee[ds] manager Howard Wilkinson in early 1992, he seemed to have burned most of his bridges [in] France.

A lucky phone call was the catalyst for Cantona's £1m transfer to United following [a] brief Leeds career during which the Frenchman had added inspiration to a team founded [on] perspiration. Most Manchester United fans recognised Cantona's class, his decisive role in Lee[ds'] 1992 title triumph and his instant hero status among Yorkshiremen. Yet few could have anticipate[d] the quality that would shine through following his arrival at Old Trafford.

For 26 years Manchester United fans had suffered under the jack boot of Liverpoo[l] domination of European and domestic trophies. Cowed into submission, their fans tended [to] hope for the best but feared the worst, even 6 seasons of relative success under Ferguson hadn[']t changed that mindset. Cantona's fearless attitude transformed the club, almost in an instan[t.] Never has a football club been so altered from one day to the next by one signing. Never has [a] club gone from 'nearly men' to 'champions' at the stroke of a pen. All of a sudden, the boot w[as] on the other foot and remains so to this day. over 10 years since Eric last kicked a ball in ange[r.]

The Complete Eric Cantona details every game Eric played for Manchester United, Lee[ds] United and the French national team as well as potted summaries of his career in France. Darre[n] Phillips, author of The Complete George Best, has painstakingly researched his remarkable care[er] in France, England and in the French national team. The Complete Eric Cantona can be rea[d] either as a work of reference or a detailed insight into a career that altered the dynamics with[in] English football for good.

THE COMPLETE
GEORGE BEST

EVERY GAME - EVERY GOAL

BY DARREN PHILLIPS

ISBN: 1901746518

£10.95 - Softback - 330 pp

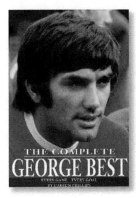

GEORGE BEST IS widely regarded as the finest footballer ever produced by the British Isles. His death in November 2005 prompted lengthy analysis of his career and his standing in the game, a debate The Complete George Best will seek to settle.

Known primarily for his rock n'roll lifestyle, this book attempts to shed more light on his often overlooked football career which was, after all, the source of his fame. Taking in every first class match George played for Manchester United and Northern Ireland with lengthy analysis of his later career in America and Fulham, The Complete George Best traces a career that caught light in the mid-sixties and burned brightly for the next 7 seasons.

Many claimed that Best was the pre-eminent player in the world during this period, his performance against Benfica in Lisbon, when he inspired United to a 5-1 win is widely regarded as the turning point for the Ulsterman, after which life was never quite the same as first the birds and then the booze followed fame into Best's life.

Best's career was inextricably linked with the fortunes of Manchester United in the 60s and Matt Busby's quest for the European Cup following the tragedy of the Munich Air disaster. United's run to the European Cup Final of 1968 saw Best a marked man. By this stage his talent was well-known and George came to life in the semi-final against Real Madrid, scoring in the first leg and setting up an unlikely winner for Bill Foulkes in the second. The final will always be remembered for Best's brilliant goal just minutes into extra time when he found space on the left and skinned the last man before rounding the 'keeper.

Most people regard the European triumph as the beginning of the end. In hindsight, and with medals the sole measure of a career's worth, then it probably was, yet Best was good enough to thrill crowds well into the next decade with famous performances such as his double hat-trick against Northampton on a muddy pitch in 1970 and a famous hat-trick against Southampton a year later. Sadly, alcholism robbed us of the best of George but most players would kill for a career record that read 639 appearances, 229 goals.

The Complete George Best is ideal both as a work of reference and a detailed insight into the great man's career. Darren Phillips has painstakingly pieced together every game and goal scored by Best from his first team debut against West Bromwich Albion in September 1963.

BACK FROM THE BRINK
by Justin Blundell
The Untold story of Manchester United
in the Depression Years 1919-32

SPECIAL OFFER: £8

If Manchester United revelled in innocent childhood during the Edwardian winning two league titles and an FA Cup within 9 years of the club's establishment endured a painful adolescence as the inter-war years saw it absent from the honc lists. In this amusing, irreverent and fascinating account, Justin Blundell traces events of the club's lost youth between the end of the Great War and the worldw economic crisis that almost scuppered the club yet ushered in a new era under Jar Gibson.

Blundell's punchy account deserves to stand alongside the many volumes writ about the post-war glory years - it tells the story of how United survived Depression Years and came back from the brink.

Memories... Of a Failed Footballer
AND A CRAP JOURNALIST
BY PAUL HINCE

PAUL HINCE BEGAN his football career with boyhood heroes Manchester City under the legendary Mercer-Allison partnership of the late 1960s before continuing his first class football career at Charlton, Bury and Crewe Alexandra. After retiring from the game he worked his way up to the heights of Manchester Evening News Manchester City correspondent and, later, that paper's first, and only, 'Chief Sports Writer'. Famed in later years for getting up the noses of both United and City fans in equal measure courtesy of his weekly columns, Paul retired from the Manchester Evening News in 2006.

SPECIAL OFFER £7

From Goal line to Touch-line
My Career with Manchester United
by Jack Crompton

Jack Crompton is one of the surviving members of Manchester United's swashbuck 1948 FA Cup winning side and the first to pen his autobiography. Jack served the clu goalkeeper, trainer and caretaker manager for over 40 years playing a major part in triumphs of the immediate post-war years and witnessed the rise of the Busby Ba first hand before leaving for a coaching role with Luton Town in 1956.

Now a sprightly octagenarian, Jack is in a unique position to discuss the considera changes in the game during his lifetime and look back on a seven decade long associat with Manchester United.

SPECIAL OFFER £12

18 TIMES AND THAT'S A FACT!
BY JUSTIN BLUNDELL
400PP - PAPERBACK - £10.95

This was the season when Sir Alex Ferguson's long-held wish to 'knock Liverpool off their f**king perch' was made flesh. A season so successful that even European Cup Final defeat to Barcelona couldn't fully diminish the club's achievements. Justin Blundell tells the story of United's triumphs in a punchy, rabidly red-eyed review of every single match and goal.

Written with an eye for the humour and pomoposity surrounding the modern game, Justin Blundell brings the matches, goals and managerial spats back to life in an entertaining, minute-by-minute guide to the matches that really mattered. "18 times" is a book for everyone who lives and breathes United, not just on match day but every single day.

SPECIAL OFFER: £8

COMPLETIST'S DELIGHT - THE FULL EMPIRE BACK LIST

ISBN	TITLE	AUTHOR	PRICE	STATUS[†]
1901746003	SF Barnes: His Life and Times	A Searle	£14.95	IP
1901746011	Chasing Glory	R Grillo	£7.95	IP
190174602X	Three Curries and a Shish Kebab	R Bott	£7.99	IP
1901746038	Seasons to Remember	D Kirkley`	£6.95	IP
1901746046	Cups For Cock-Ups+	A Shaw	£8.99	OOP
1901746054	Glory Denied	R Grillo	£8.95	IP
1901746062	Standing the Test of Time	B Alley	£16.95	IP
1901746070	The Encyclopaedia of Scottish Cricket	D Potter	£9.99	IP
1901746089	The Silent Cry	J MacPhee	£7.99	OOP
1901746097	The Amazing Sports Quiz Book	F Brockett	£6.99	IP
1901746100	I'm Not God, I'm Just a Referee	R Entwistle	£7.99	OOP
1901746119	The League Cricket Annual Review 2000	ed. S. Fish	£6.99	IP
1901746143	Roger Byrne - Captain of the Busby Babes	I McCartney	£16.95	OOP
1901746151	The IT Manager's Handbook	D Miller	£24.99	IP
190174616X	Blue Tomorrow	M Meehan	£9.99	IP
1901746178	Atkinson for England	G James	£5.99	IP
1901746186	Think Cricket	C Bazalgette	£6.00	IP
1901746194	The League Cricket Annual Review 2001	ed. S. Fish	£7.99	IP
1901746208	Jock McAvoy - Fighting Legend *	B Hughes	£9.95	IP
1901746216	The Tommy Taylor Story*	B Hughes	£8.99	OOP
1901746224	Willie Pep*+	B Hughes	£9.95	OOP
1901746232	For King & Country*+	B Hughes	£8.95	OOP
1901746240	Three In A Row	P Windridge	£7.99	IP
1901746259	Viollet - Life of a legendary goalscorer+PB	R Cavanagh	£16.95	OOP
1901746267	Starmaker	B Hughes	£16.95	IP
1901746283	Morrissey's Manchester	P Gatenby	£5.99	IP
1901746313	Sir Alex, United & Me	A Pacino	£8.99	IP
1901746321	Bobby Murdoch, Different Class	D Potter	£10.99	OOP
190174633X	Goodison Maestros	D Hayes	£5.99	OOP
1901746348	Anfield Maestros	D Hayes	£5.99	OOP
1901746364	Out of the Void	B Yates	£9.99	IP
1901746356	The King - Denis Law, hero of the...	B Hughes	£17.95	OOP
1901746372	The Two Faces of Lee Harvey Oswald	G B Fleming	£8.99	IP
1901746380	My Blue Heaven	D Friend	£10.99	IP
1901746399	Viollet - life of a legendary goalscorer	B Hughes	£11.99	IP
1901746402	Quiz Setting Made Easy	J Dawson	£7.99	IP
1901746410	The Insider's Guide to Manchester United	J Doherty	£20	IP
1901746437	Catch a Falling Star	N Young	£17.95	IP
1901746453	Birth of the Babes	T Whelan	£12.95	OOP
190174647X	Back from the Brink	J Blundell	£10.95	IP
1901746488	The Real Jason Robinson	D Swanton	£17.95	IP
1901746496	This Simple Game	K Barnes	£14.95	IP
1901746518	The Complete George Best	D Phillips	£10.95	IP
1901746526	From Goalline to Touch line	J Crompton	£16.95	IP
1901746534	Sully	A Sullivan	£8.95	IP
1901746542	Memories...	P Hince	£10.95	IP
1901746550	Reminiscences of Manchester	L Hayes	£12.95	IP
1901746569	Morrissey's Manchester - 2nd Ed.	P Gatenby	£8.95	IP
1901746577	The Story of the Green & Gold	C Boujaoude	£10.95	IP
1901746585	The Complete Eric Cantona	D Phillips	£10.95	IP
1901746593	18 Times	J Blundell	£9.95	IP
1901746 607	Old Trafford - 100 Years	I McCartney	£12.95	IP
1901746615	Remember Me	K C Kanjilal	£7.95	IP
1901746623	The Villa Premier Years	S Brookes	£8.95	IP
1901746631	Broken Youth	K Woods	£8.95	IP
190174664X	The Devil's Dust	B Yates	£9.95	IP
1901746658	Grafting for England	T Sullivan	£8.95	I{
1901746666	The Carpet King of Texas	P Kennedy	£8.95	IP
1901746704	Manchester United Premier Years	S Brookes	£8.95	IP

* Originally published by Collyhurst & Moston Lads Club + Out of print PB Superceded by Paperback edition

[†] In Print/Out Of Print/To Be Published (date)